THE
EXCITING
JOURNEY
of a
VILLAGE
BOY

ATREYAPURAM
TO
MUMBAI MEGAPOLIS

THE
EXCITING
JOURNEY
of a
VILLAGE
BOY

A Father's Legacy

Dr. Kasichainula Kameswara Rao

CINNAMONTEAL
DESIGN & PUBLISHING

First published in India in 2019 by CinnamonTeal Publishing

Copyright © 2019 Kasichainula Kameswara Rao

ISBN 978–93–87676–20–6

BISAC Code: BIO026000/Biography & Autobiography/Personal Memoirs

Cover conceptualization: Suryanarayan Kasichainula

Book and cover design: CinnamonTeal Design and Publishing

CinnamonTeal Publishing
an imprint of CinnamonTeal Design & Publishing
Plot No 16, Housing Board Colony
Gogol, Margao
Goa 403601 India
www.cinnamonteal.in

This book is dedicated to my father
Shri Kasichainula Suryanarayana

Preface

ৡ

The world has changed fast and so have occupations and places of living. The traditional joint family has slowly changed to nuclear families due to changes in education system and migration to corporate and private jobs from traditional agrarian dependence and vedic education. In the process, keeping track of one's origins and ancestry has become difficult. I had the benefit of knowing our ancestry as a young child from my parents and relatives. I had to move out of my native place after high school education and out of state for post-graduation and employment. My children also migrated out of Mumbai for education and employment. I, therefore, thought that I should record our family history and my experiences of life for the benefit of the next generations.

I have been thinking about the structure and contents for some time. I could not arrive at a specific format. My wife and I were holidaying in the USA with my second son, Gopal Kasichainula in May 2010. During the course of my narration of incidents, my daughter-in-law, Radhika gave me a book, "A father's legacy: Your life story in your own words". This book provided ideas for development of the theme to record my story. The events are too many and I recorded to the extent possible. Apart from my own experiences, the story briefly covers eight generations of our "Kasichainula' family.

I targeted to complete it for the golden jubilee function of our marriage. It was ready in draft form. The function was organized on June 12, 2017 to suit the conveniences of our children and grandchildren. I am thankful to Shri. N. N. Murty Garu, father in-law of my daughter Lakshmi Nukala for agreeing to unveil the story and for saying encouraging and pleasant words. The function was organized at our home in Navi Mumbai, India.

My eldest son, Suryanarayan Kasichainula has been instrumental in making this book available in print and digital format.

K. Kameswara Rao
June 12, 2017
D-15, Kalapatru CHS Ltd.
Sector 8B, CBD Belapur,
Navi Mumbai, Maharashtra
dr_kkrao@yahoo.com

Acknowledgements

৩৩

I thank Selma Davis for her patience and dedication in converting the written manuscript of this book. I also thank Yorke Communications Pvt. Ltd. for their support in completing this book.

Contents

ౡ

Contents

The Kasichainulas of Atreyapuram

ೞ

In the present-day East Godavari district of Andhra Pradesh lies a land that's akin to paradise. A very popular 'Telugu' poet, Srinadha, who served as an education officer in an ancient kingdom in the region liked the place very much. So much so that he described the land—abound with rivers, lakes, fruit and flower gardens, and temples—as one that had no comparison on earth.

The mighty Godavari river flows through this district and its neighbouring West Godavari district. The Godavari splits into two major rivers—Gautami and Vasishta—after Rajahmundry. Nestled between the two rivers, this land is very fertile, with orchards overflowing with mangoes, coconuts, bananas, and other fruits, lush paddy fields, and bountiful crops growing on agricultural plots. There is no shortage of water at any time of the year. This land is known as the Godavari Central Delta.

The Kasichainulas of Atreyapuram

Over the years, many villages came up in the area because of its conducive location, abundant supply of water, and fertile land. One such village was Atreyapuram, 25 km from Rajahmundry, on the banks of the Gautami river. According to legend, the village derived its name from Atri Maharishi, who meditated on the banks of the river in ancient times. Even today, the peepal tree under which he is believed to have meditated stands tall.

Because of the many advantages of the land, its peaceful environment, and lack of social unrest, ancient scholars with knowledge of Sanskrit, the Vedas, yagnas, and yagas were attracted to the region. As they flourished here, many Vedic agraharams—a Brahmin neighbourhood in a village consisting of row houses on either side of the road—came up with grants from local rulers. Atreyapuram too has such agraharam.

Sir Arthur Cotton, a British engineer who devoted his life to building irrigation and navigation canals in 19th-century India, further improved water resources in the delta by constructing anicuts on the river around 150 years ago; these anicuts were later converted into barrages, enabling multiple cropping throughout the year in the region. Agriculture, is the main occupation of the people, while dairy farming is also popular.

In our community in Andhra Pradesh, people are identified by the region to which they belong. Our ancestors were supposed to hail from Kosala Desa. They were known as the Kosalyas or Kasalanati sakha. Some of them migrated from Kosala Desa and initially settled in present-day Madhya Pradesh (Chhattisgarh), Orissa, and Telangana.

There is an interesting story behind the origin of our surname, Kasichainula. Our ancestors are said to have performed a yagna by name of Chayanam in Kasi, i.e., Varanasi. Hence the surname.

The Kasichainulas were all great scholars of Sanskrit, the Vedas, performance of pujas, and yagnas, and acted as ritriks and purohits, and also good agriculturists. The Kasichainula family's Gothra is Kaundinyasa. The family is triarisheya-vasista, Mytravaruna and Kaundinya.

A family of three brothers arrived at this place around the year 1740. The oldest of them, Shri. Kasichainula Nrisimha Somayajulu, settled down in Atreyapuram while the other two brothers chose to live in the nearby villages of Nadavapalli and Kothalanka.

Nrisimha was respected as a great scholar of Sanskrit Vedic texts, Purohitam, and related areas. He was also a rich man who had acquired large tracts of land in and around the village and was known to have gold, silver, and money. He was reputed to be broad-minded, very generous—he was always helping people in need—kind-hearted and dignified. He was also tall, fair, and handsome.

Around that time, an interesting incident occurred. An idol made of red sandalwood came floating in the Gautami river. It got caught in the net of a fisherman, who handed it over to the elders of Vadapalli village, just 2 km from Atreyapuram. At first, they couldn't decide whose idol it was. Then Nrisimha and some other scholars concluded that it was the idol of Lord Venkateswara. The news reached the local Maharaja. Vadapalli fell under the jurisdiction of Peddapuram Sansthan.

Raja Timma Jagapathi Raju constructed a beautiful temple for Lord Venkateswara and donated about 275 acres of land for its maintenance, besides paying the salaries of the staff. In keeping with the tradition, Vaishnava Iyengars were appointed as priests. Nrisimha was appointed the Raj Purohit.

Nrisimha had one son and three daughters. His son, Shri. Sundarama Somayajulu, like his father, was a great scholar, well respected in the village and the neighbourhood. He performed Vedic ritual Somayagam and acquired the official title of Yagneswara Somayaji. He had two daughters, Sathemma and Varalakshamma, but no sons. He, therefore, adopted his father's brother's grandson, Shri. Jagannadha Somayajulu. He too grew up to have a great reputation, like his father and grandfather.

Jagannadha had no children from his first marriage. The elders decided to get him remarried and, accordingly, he got married to Venkusodemma in the French territory of Yanam. When the wedding party returned home, his first wife, who did not know about his second marriage, questioned him about his dress and the Paranni on his feet. He told her that he had remarried for children. She, made him promise that he would name his first child after her. Jagannadha promised her that all the children born to him would be named after her. Accordingly, Somayajulu named his five children from his second wife as Jagannadha Sarma, Jaganadham, Peda Jaggamma, Chinna Jaggamma, and Bulli Jaggamma.

Jagannadha's elder sister, Varalakshamma, was reputed to be very beautiful. It is said that the deity in the local Mahalakshmi temple is sculptured on seeing her. The temple is still there, and thousands visit it every year. During Chaitra Masa, an annual festival is performed at the temple and people offer mangoes and other agriculture produce to the deity. It was a childhood ritual for us to visit the temple every year.

Jagannadha Sarma was our grandfather. He was liberal in thought and a great leader. People flocked to him wherever he went. He was a reputed scholar of the Vedas, Sanskrit, and Telugu, but he did not pursue the traditional family profession. Instead, he chose to become a full-time agriculturist. He planted fruit trees on 12 acres of land—four acres each of mango, sapota, and mosambi orchards. He also planted other varieties of fruit trees. On another 60 acres, he cultivated rice, dals like tur, urad and moong, jawar, til, and a variety of vegetables. To water the trees, he dug a huge well, which was there till recently. Ironically, he never enjoyed the fruits of his labour as he died before the trees started yielding fruit. He died at the age of 28 due to typhoid, which was not curable at that time.

On April 15, 1904, Jagannadha Sarma was blessed with a son named Suryanarayana. Suryanarayana was just eight years when he lost his father. It was also at a bad time. My father was about to be admitted to a high school in a neighbouring district where their close relative was the headmaster. After my grandfather's death, my grandmother did not want to send him away from home for education. So, he continued his studies in Sanskrit, Telugu, and received traditional education.

My father grew up with a cousin brother and two cousin sisters. The brother's name was Subrahmanyam. My father was having the nickname of 'Pedda Kaschellu or Kasulu' and my uncle 'Chinna Kaschellu or Kasulu'. In fact, most of the villagers, even today, are familiar with the nicknames only. The two were so thick that everyone thought of them as real brothers. In fact, for many years, we too believed the same. Similarly, his cousin sisters treated him as their own brother and he treated them like his own sisters. Such was familial affection in those days.

Atreyapuram Agraharam was originally on the banks of the Gautami river, which was convenient for the daily rituals of its residents. However, a devastating flood in 1880 destroyed the agraharam and all the houses were submerged in the river. The residents then started searching for an alternate place to live in. A Vysya donor, Shri. Yelamarti Bangarayya, offered them the present-day site, which was a furlong away from the old one but still close enough to the river for the people to do their daily rituals. Residential plots were given to all and they constructed new pakka houses. Our ancestral house was constructed by my grandfather's grandfather, Shri. Sundarama Somayajulu. It was the largest and the most beautiful house in the area, with a front house, followed by a verandah and a large manduva house.

Our ancestors from my mother's side had migrated to Atreyapuram, much earlier, in the year 1606 from Golconda kingdom. One of their ancestors, Shri. Anantha Padmanabha Paudarika Somayajulu, was an outstanding Vedic scholar during the reign of Muhammad Quli Qutub Shah, the Nawab of Golconda, a great patron of scholars from different fields. Every year, the Nawab used to honour accomplished scholars in the tradition of the Hampi Vijayanagar kings. He chose to honour Shri. Anantha Padmanabha and conferred him the title of Jatavallabha, as he was outstanding in the Jata path of the Vedas. In due course, Jatavallabhula became their surname. Their original surname was Vedurucharla.

In subsequent years, life in Golconda became difficult due to law and order problems. Most of the residents left the place, but

Paudarika was reluctant to do so. However, he advised his children to leave for safer places. His second son, Shri. Ramabhadra Somayajulu, chose Atreyapuram as it would be convenient for his daily anustanam (rituals). Atreyapuram was under the Peddapuram kingdom. Golconda and Peddapuram were friendly neighbours and so he migrated to Atreyapuram Agraharam in 1606.

My father was born almost 300 years after their migration. My grandfather, Jagannadha Sarma, and Shri. Jatavallabhula Krishna Somayajulu were contemporaries; my grandfather was married to the latter's sister, Kameswaramma. Marrying one's maternal uncle's daughter was a norm in our society.

The time came for my father's marriage. He had two maternal uncles. The younger uncle had a son and a daughter who was fair and beautiful. The elder uncle, Krishna Somayajulu, had six sons and four daughters. My grandmother chose Krishna's daughter because she came from a large family. She felt that in Kasichainula families, there were very few children and she wanted my father to have many children. Accordingly, the match was fixed. Financially, Krishna was no match for the Kasichainula family. But he felt he should perform a five-day marriage in keeping with my family's status. The wedding was a grand affair, but left Krishna financially drained.

In 1926, my father's elders decided to divide the family property between him and his uncle. My father was given a compensation of Rs.600 to construct a new house. His uncle retained the ancestral house. My father acquired a plot of land nearby and constructed a new house. He shifted there in August 1927. They divided the landed property of 70 acres equally after disposing off lands in far-off places. Their original land holding was much more.

My maternal grandfather Sri Krishna Somayajulu was as outstanding Vedic scholar capable of conducting sophisticated Vedic rituals single handedly. He was appointed trustee of the Vadapalli Devasthanam. He ran it well, except in one case, where he was caught unaware. He had purchased two acres of land in a different place for the Devasthanam without the approval of the British authorities. They ordered him to sell off the land and deposit the money in the temple account. He could not do it, so the authorities proceeded to prosecute him. My father bailed him out by borrowing money from various sources.

Thus, my father was under financial stress due to the construction of the house, bailing out his maternal uncle, and additional expenses because of participation in the freedom movement. The Great Depression of 1929-33 had a severely adverse economic impact the world over, with asset prices crashing and incomes declining steeply. My father too had to bear its impact. Under pressure from lenders, he had to sell 10 acres of land, a third of his landed property, to repay an outstanding loan of Rs. 3,000. Some people advised that he repay just part of the loan, like his friends had done during the freedom struggle by transferring the land to their spouses' names. He felt it was unethical and did not do so. In the intervening period, some of his relatives unleashed a propaganda as they wanted him to lose his land as well as his house. Ironically, most of them were beneficiaries of his benevolence. After selling off 10 acres, he still had 20 acres of land. Then there was our big, beautiful house with its tiled roof, two big halls, three bedrooms, and three small rooms with sitouts in the front and at the back.

We are five brothers and six sisters. Large families were a norm in those days and they were honored. Unfortunately, my eldest brother, Jaganath Sarma died when he was 22 years old due to typhoid fever. He had just completed his sanitary inspector course and awaiting his job appointment. He was married. My younger sister Sitalaxmi died very early due to consequences of a near fatal accident when she was three years old. My eldest brother, Dr. K. Krishna Murthy retired as medical officer of Kakinada Municipality. He later continued to be a very popular doctor. My younger brother K. Sundararam did M.A. (Economics). He started as a banker and later moved to the private sector. Our youngest brother, Dr. K. Venkateshwarlu did his PhD. in Engineering from Canada and retired from an international company. One of our sisters' Vasa Prabhavati is a PhD. in Telugu literature. She is an orator and a popular writer. Other four sisters, Bhavanibhatla Suryakantam, Kolapalli Ramalakshmi, Missula Ratnavati and Katakam Varalakshmi are housewives.

My father had joined the Congress party as a volunteer at the young age of 17. At that time, Congress meetings were held at Kakinada. He actively participated in the Salt Satyagraha in 1931 and the Quit India Movement in 1942. He was arrested and put in Rajahmundry Central Jail. Some of the Congress leaders who visited our house during the freedom movement were Jayaprakash Narayan, Tanguturi Prakasam, Bulusu Sambamurti, Kala Venkata Rao, Durgabai Deshmukh, and Madduri Annapoormayya, to name a few. One of my elder sisters was born in 1938 when Jayaprakash visited our house. She was named Prabhavati, after JP's wife. My grandmother was an excellent cook and she used to prepare wonderful dishes for all the guests.

After India's Independence, my father became the president of Kothapeta Taluka Congress and continued in the post for 10 years. Later, he was appointed the district Congress election officer for life. Shri M.V.S. Subbaraju was the general secretary who later became an MLA and government chief whip. They were close throughout. In fact, he was close to my elder brother and me too. He was like our family member. The split in the INC left my father very disappointed and hurt.

My father had a large role to play in the contribution to the development of our village and neighbourhood. He was instrumental in getting the electrification proposal sanctioned by the relevant minister. He also got approvals for a high school, a hospital, and a cooperative bank. He helped many in getting jobs as teachers and helped students get admission in polytechnic institutes. Above all, he helped many people, including our close relatives, financially during their time of need.

Of mangoes, melas, and Makar Sankranti

ॐ

Childhood is the most interesting and carefree stage of a person's life. The environment, of course, has a great impact on a child. Atreyapuram, as mentioned earlier, was on the banks of the Gautami river with a small population of 2000- 3000. It was the firca (a part of taluka) headquarters. Originally, it was called Razole taluka and later became Kothapeta taluka. It had canal as well as borewell irrigation. Rice was the staple crop, but it grew only once a year. Jowar, tur, urad, moong, and til were the other crops grown there. Tobacco and banana were the major commercial crops. There were many fruit and vegetable orchards.

The Central Godavari Delta area was surrounded by rivers. People had to cross the Godavari at Rajahmundry by steamer or boat to travel to the villages, which was not possible after sunset. In other areas, one could cross the Gautami or the Vasishta by boats, which were again not operational after sunset. Sir Arthur Cotton had constructed anicuts at Dhavaleswaram, Bobbarlanka, and Vijjeswaram, but they were only for irrigation and were not motorable. In the summer, when there was no water, some people would cross the dam by vehicles, unauthorised.

The water needs of households were met with water from wells or handpumps. There was a canal for irrigation. There was also a large tank in the middle of the village which was used for various purposes. Thus, there was no shortage of water. There were two rainy seasons—the southwest monsoon and the northeast monsoon, which was not so severe. During the southwest monsoon, there was danger of flooding in the Godavari, so huge bunds were built to control the floods.

There was only one main road which was paved; all others were mud roads. In the rainy season, they were difficult to navigate. There was no electricity. Kerosene lamps were the only source of light. There are four main temples, dedicated to Lord Shiva, Lord Vishnu, and two to Mahalakshmi Ammavaru.

Diverse communities lived peacefully in Atreyapuram. Originally, it was the military garage of the Peddapuram Raja. Therefore, a large number of people belonging to the Kshatriya Community (Rajus) lived there. Their main occupation was agriculture in peaceful times. Veda recitation and performing pujas and yagnas were the occupation of the priestly clans in the Agraharam. Wealthy local rulers supported and encouraged them. Business and trade were carried by the trading community. Traders, who were generally rich, were the local moneylenders. Agricultural operations needed the support of artisan communities like blacksmiths, potters, barbers, toddy tappers, washer men and large agricultural labourers. There was a fishermen's colony on the banks of the river. There was one popular doctor and some Ayurvedic physicians in the village. Babies were delivered at home with help from local midwives when needed.

When I was born, India and the world were going through a very active and vibrant period. On one hand, World War II was on and on the other, the movement for India's Independence led by the INC was buoyant.

I was born on May 23, 1942, Saturday, at 06:10 A at my father's house in my paternal village, Atreyapuram. According to the Hindu calendar, it was Jyeshta masa, Shukla Paksha, and the tithi was Ashtami.

I was the third son of my parents. I had two brothers and four sisters, elder to me. According to our family tradition, on the 11th or 21st day after the birth of a baby, a function known as Balasala is organised, in which the child's horoscope is drawn and a name is given. Such a function was held for me as well.

My two elder brothers were named after my paternal and maternal grandfathers. In my case, my paternal grandmother exercised her choice. She didn't want her name to be given to any of my sisters, as she was widowed at a young age. I was fair and healthy like my grandfather, so she decided that I should be named after her. I was named Kameswara Rao after Kameswaramma. Rao was imported from Maharashtra, perhaps inspired by the bravery of the Peshwas. However, my nickname was Kamudu and people used to call me by that name. Next was the drawing of the horoscope, called the Jataka Chakra. One of our distant relatives, Shri. Chitti Kamayya, was a renowned astrologer. He drew my horoscope. According to him, I would grow up to be well-educated, well to do, would enjoy life, have a good family life, and, above all, be a good speaker. But as a child, I was very shy, timid, an introvert, and hardly communicative!

My earliest memories are from the time I was three years old. I faintly remember my grandmother, after whom I was named. I remember that my father used to take me to our gardens and the annual teertham (festival) to the Lord Venkateswara temple. In our tradition, the father is the first guru (teacher) of the child. His first lesson was Sanskrit Shlokas. Accordingly, my father, taught me the Telugu alphabet, the numbers 1 to 100, and the names of the seven weekdays, 12 months, 27 nakshatras, and 60 years as per the Hindu calendar, and so on. He would teach me mostly at night and I would fall asleep listening to him. My memory was sharp, and I learnt things fast.

Our house was constructed on an-almost 1,200 square yard plot with a built-up area of 3,000 sq. ft. There was a front courtyard, a bigger back courtyard, and a third courtyard beyond a compound wall. The house had two big halls, three bedrooms, three small rooms, an open area called arugu and another one at the back. From the north side of the house, there were closed lanes leading to the backyard.

One big hall was used as a drawing room and the other as the dining room. Cooking was done adjoining to this room. One of the small rooms in the front was used as a storage room for bins filled with paddy for the entire year. Another small front room was used as a library called Sarad Grandhalayam started by my father along with his friends during the freedom movement. My father's room was on the east side; the two other bedrooms were used by other family members. The small room at the rear of the house was known as the chittugadhi—it was the nursing room where all of us brothers and sisters were born. At other times, it was used for pounding of paddy into rice and for other purposes.

In the front courtyard, there was a big malati creeper that used to flower during the rainy season, close to Vinayak Chaturthi. There were other flowering plants as well. The rear courtyard was used to grow vegetables like brinjal, lady's finger, different kinds of gourd, beans, etc. It also had fruit trees like orange, sweet lime, and grapes. My father would grow and tend to them. He had a special interest in flowering plants and he grew parijat, sampang, night queen, gurasham kanakambaram, mandar, marigold, chamanti, maruvom, dhavanam, and so on. There were three coconut trees, one of which was a gangabandam tree, which has extremely sweet water. Our homegrown vegetables sufficed most of our needs and the only thing we purchased was potatoes. In the outer courtyard, there was a cattle shed for buffaloes and cows who used to feed on dry and green grass, bran, grains, etc. We also had jackfruit and sitaphal trees.

My father was very particular that the house should be always neat and clean, and the servants followed his instructions meticulously. He himself was always well-dressed—wearing a spotless white khadi dhoti, full-sleeved shirt, and an angavastram on his shoulder. His clothes were always well-ironed and he wore spectacles. Whenever any office-bearers of the Congress or other leaders of the freedom movement visited our house, lunch would be arranged for them. Some would come seeking favours from ministers and other influential people well-known to my father. He had very close contacts with Shri. Kala Venkata Rao and Shri. S.S.P. Pattabhi Rama Rao, both ministers in the government. Almost all the MLAs and MP's in the district were close to him and respected him as he was considered to be a sincere party activist.

Once Shri. Kala Venkata Rao came to our house and as the youngest member of the family, I was asked to garland him. He was very tall, so he bent down and accepted the garland from me. I had a similar experience with Shri. Pattabhi Rama Rao.

Whenever my father was in the village, the house would be full of visitors. These were Congress party workers to discuss party matters & receive instructions, relatives, or people seeking favors. He used to help all. He would never boast about what he did for others. He always wanted his children to have good habits. He rarely scolded us, at most he would give us a warning look. My father used to smile and laugh heartily.

My mother's name was Lakshmidevamma but both family and villagers called her Ammadu, her nickname. Having been married off early, she would assist her mother-in-law and other elders of the family in various tasks. She was intelligent and had abundant common sense. Nobody needed to tell her what to do. Having come from an educated family, she was well-versed in Sanskrit, religious customs, puja methods, and the traditions of our society. She had perfected cooking to an art form. She knew what each person in the family liked and would cook delectable savoury and sweet dishes for us. She was a devoted wife and ably assisted my father in his activities related to the freedom movement and other social matters. Her six brothers had special regard for her and whenever they visited our house, she took special care of them.

She would tend to the cattle and milk the buffaloes and cows, both morning and evening. She would then boil the milk on a fire made by burning cow dung cakes, prepare curd, buttermilk, butter, and ghee. We never ran out of dairy products. We also had a full-time servant to look after the cattle.

When villagers would come to her with small ailments, she would give them medicines which she used to bring from her doctor brother. People often came to her asking for milk, curd, vegetables, rice, and pulses. She was always generous to them. Some would seek religious advice from her. Whenever a function or festival took place, she would be invited and we would accompany her. We used to regularly visit the Madiki village across the Godavari, where my father's aunt lived, Kakinada, my maternal uncle's home, and Tuni, my eldest sister's place.

Our childhood days in our village were very happy and without a care. We used to play games like chedugudu (kabaddi), chor-police, monkey game, gilli-danda (cricket), and race with each other. We used to play games like golibilla and bongaram in secret as the elders wouldn't allow us to play them as these games were played by the Servants. In the summer months, we use to have to palmyra fruits and raw mangoes and go to the Godavari river for baths and boat rides. I was a reasonably good climber and would climb up coconut and palmyra trees. I was also good at swimming.

During my growing up days, there were no boys of my age for me to play with. All my peers were girls. Therefore, all my male friends were either older or younger than me. But that was never a problem.

One of our most enjoyable annual activities as kids was going to the Vadapalli Teertham. Every year in April, the Kalyanotsavam of Lord Venkateswara used to take place. During that time, a huge three-day mela (festival) was held, which would often run into 10 days. We used to look forward to going to the mela, just 2 km from our village, in a bullock cart. The cart and the two bullocks pulling it were specially decorated for the occasion. There was a festive look everywhere. It was a time for revelry—we would gorge on snacks and sweets, play games, ride rangula ratnam, get photographs taken, watch magic shows, etc., at the festival. The mela drew people from both nearby villages and far-off places. Apart from the Kalyanotsavam, a major attraction was the Radhosthavam (chariot drawing). My father was the managing trustee of the temple.

The summer months were enjoyable in many other ways. It was the time the mango trees planted by our grandfather were laden with fruit. There was a wide variety of mangoes—some had flavourful juices, some were good for cutting and eating, others were meant to be eaten raw or to be made into pickles. The varieties that were good for eating were brought home in batches and covered with paddy straw and left to ripen. We would eat the juicy varieties—chinnarasam, kothapalli kobbari, suvarnarekha, panchadharakalasa—by popping them into our mouth and squeezing out the juice. Other varieties like banaganapalle and cherukurasam were for cutting and eating. Whenever my father was at home, he would peel skin and cut mangoes into pieces and distribute them among us to eat. We were not encouraged to eat raw mangoes as they can cause stomach aches or indigestion, especially in children. They were to be eaten sparingly and with chilli powder and salt. We also had other kinds of fruits like sapota (chickoo), mosambi (sweet lime), and jackfruit in abundance.

While most of my childhood was happy, I remember two events that shook me up, both natural calamities. One was the severe cyclone of 1949. The winds, accompanied by heavy rain, were so strong that trees were uprooted and many buildings were destroyed. A coconut tree fell on our house, the compound wall was flattened, and there was some damage to one side of the house. The other incident was the Godavari floods of 1953. Many villages were submerged and thousands of acres of crops were totally damaged. Young men would keep a round-the-clock vigil as there were rumours that downstream villagers were planning to cut the Godavari bund in the upstream villages so that the impact of the floods on them was less. Of course, nothing like that happened.

Every summer, the making of pickles was a major activity. In Andhra households, pickles are an essential part of the daily lunch/dinner menu. My mother would make at least 10 varieties of pickles every year. The most popular ones were avakai, magai, menthikai, turpu avakai, puliharavakai, tokkudu pachadi, persaravakai, etc. Normally, households made only five types, but my mother made many more varieties in order to cater to everyone's tastes. In addition, she would make and preserve uppu baddhalu—salted dried mango chips—for the year. These pickles are stored in big mud pots and eaten throughout the year. Over time, ceramic jars replaced the mud pots.

Another important childhood experience for us was the celebration of festivals. The four most important festivals were

Ganesh Chaturthi, Dasara, Deepavali, and Makar Sankranti. The fifth one is Ugadi, but it falls during the annual examinations, so celebrations are low key. Ganesh Chaturthi usually falls in August/September. When we were kids, there were no readymade Ganesh idols available. So, we had them made to order. An elderly person by the name of Guni Brahmam used to make idols in our village. These idols had to be prepared only with soil from snake pits. For the puja rituals, we would collect a variety of leaves and flowers such as bilva, semi, and gilledu. Our malati creeper used to flower around that time and we had plenty of flowers. My mother would cook a special lunch of Undrallu and a sweetmeat called Kajjikayalu made with rice, rava, gud, and coconut. There was a canopy above the idol decorated with a variety of fruits, corn, and kaluva flowers. My father would make us do the puja while he recited the mantras. We would keep the idol for one or three days. After the puja was over, we would keep the idol in our grain bins believing that Ganesha would not allow rats to spoil the grain. The village would celebrate Ganesh Utsav en masse.

Dasara was celebrated on a bigger scale as schools and colleges would be shut for 15 days. Everyone would visit their native places during that time. Women would visit their parents with their children in tow; sometimes their husbands would join them. Everyone had to have new clothes. In those days, readymade garments were not easily available, therefore, tailors had a busy time. For students, it was important to perform Saraswati Puja for three days—Durga Ashtami, Navami and Vijayadashami. We would select some books, wrap them in paper and keep them at the place of prayer. Pujas would be done both morning and evening for three days. My father used to recite the puja path. My mother would cook special dishes on all the three days. My brothers-in-law and other close relatives would visit us. The entire village used to wear a festive look and every house was packed with guests.

Deepavali is another important festival, but unfortunately, it comes during the northeast monsoon and often the rain spoilt the festive fervour. Bursting firecrackers was the most exciting part of the festival. My father even made firecrackers at home for our enjoyment. We would buy the raw materials and chemicals and make flower pots, rockets, patas, matabas, etc. The crackers had to be dried and here the rain would play havoc. When there was no rain, we enjoyed the festival for three days.

Makar Sankranti is by far the most important festival in our region. It is generally celebrated for four days—13th, 14th, 15th, and 16th January, called Bhogi, Sankranti, Kanuma, and Mukkanuma respectively. The festival coincides with the harvest. When we were kids entire village vibrated with festive fervour— people would decorate their houses, level their front yards, and spray cow dung water on it. The women would make beautiful rangolis in a variety of colours and designs. Like during other festivals, relatives visited each other. Schools and colleges were closed for two weeks. Haridas, a folk singer, would go from door to door every day, singing songs, musical instruments in his hands. He would have a brass pot on his head to collect rice donations from people. Some people would also go around the village with decorated bulls (gangireddu) putting up shows. They too would collect clothes and rice from the villagers. Giving alms is a must during this period.

On Bhogi, we would get up early in the morning, take a bath, and make a big bonfire on every street corner. We also dropped garlands of dried cow dung cakes and the girls would sing songs circling the gobbillu amma, made out of cow dung and flowers. Makar Sankranti is the key day as on this day, the Sun God changes his path. In the Hindu calendar, this is called Uttarayana Punya Kala. All of us would bathe in the Godavari river, wear new clothes, and greet each other. My mother would cook a special lunch for all of us. Kanuma is an important day for farmers. They would decorate the bullocks used in cultivation and conduct races for them. Mukkanuma is an extension of that. It is also a day when most of the guests left for their homes.

Sports and games were very popular during the four-day festival. In our village, the most popular sport was cockfights, which were organised at designated places. The audience would bet on the winner. Of course, kids were barred from witnessing them. Once, I went secretly with our servant to see a cockfight. But I did not enjoy it as I felt it was very cruel.

The grown-up men would also play cards on all four days of the festival, laying, winning, and losing bets. There were a few other local games as well.

Sravanamasam is a very important month for ladies. Every Tuesdays and Fridays they perform special pujas and wear new clothes and jewelry. Of course, our interest is in the special dishes they would offer to eat.

In Andhra 'on all festival days' houses are decorated with mango leaves and marigold flowers.

An education, and some life lessons

ಬಿಬಿ

My first teacher in life was my father. He used to teach me alphabets and numbers 1-100 in Telugu and English. He also taught me the names of the days, weeks, and months in both the languages, besides the names of the 60 years according to the Hindu calendar. I learnt all these things by heart. He would invariably teach me all this late in the evening while I was lying beside him before we fell sleep. There were some breaks in my lessons because of his frequent journeys.

My formal education started when I turned five and joined school. In Andhra Pradesh, children have a formal introduction to the alphabet in a social ceremony called Aksharabhyasam. Students wear new clothes and tilaks on their foreheads and are given new slates and balapams (slate and pencil). On the day of my Aksharabhyasam, my teacher, Shri. Subbarao, held my hand in his and made me write Om Namah Shivaya Siddham Namaha on my slate and chanted a mantra three times. The teacher who performs the Aksharabhyasam is gifted new clothes, money, fruits, and other items. My father gifted my teacher accordingly. All the people present at the event are served sweets and snacks. The scale of the event is commensurate with the financial status of the student's family. People prefer to conduct the ritual during Dassara. It's an unforgettable day for every student.

My primary school was known as a board school, perhaps because it was administered by the East Godavari District Board. The school was a stone's throw away from our home, so we used to walk. The school is still there, though the old building has been replaced by a new one. Corporal punishment—beating with sticks, pinching, striking on the buttocks, etc.—was commonplace during those days. At times, we were made to stand on the bench, or out in the sun, and sometimes we were made to stand facing the wall.

I was a very obedient and sincere student. So, I was never meted out any such punishment. There's only one incident of disobedience that I can remember. One day, I refused to go to school for some reason. My teacher, who stayed close to our place, came to pick me up. Even then I refused to go to school. He took my hand and forcefully dragged me. I shouted at him, weeping. He refused to let go of me and finally I relented. But that day in school I did not speak to anybody, including my teacher, as I felt humiliated.

I did well from Standard I-III. I was doing well because of my sharp memory and concentration. My parents and teachers started appreciating my academic performance. In many subjects, I was at par with my seniors from Standards IV and V. My teachers met my father and told him that I could be considered for a double promotion. Accordingly, in consultation with the headmaster, I was allowed to informally attend some classes in Form I (Standard VI). In those days, direct admission to Form II (Standard VII) was allowed if one passed an entrance test. I cleared the test and was admitted to Form II. In the process, I became the youngest student in high school at that time. Standards I-V comprised primary school, while Standards VI-XI were in high school. Standard XI is known as SSLC (Secondary School Leaving Certificate).

I always did well at studies—from primary school right up to high school. I'd get either the first or the second rank in almost all subjects. The main subjects were English, Telugu, Math, Science, and Social Studies. In addition, there were craft, drawing, physical training, and Hindi. There were periodic debating classes, social service sessions, sports, picnics, etc. I was bad at debating as I was very shy and timid. The teachers tried to get me to open up and talk more.

Every year, the district education officer (DEO) used to visit the high school for an inspection. He'd visit each class and ask the students some questions. I and three of my classmates would always have the correct answers. One year, the DEO wanted some students to deliver speeches in front of all the 350 students of the school. The headmaster selected four students, including me. It was very tough for me to speak in public and I was scared, but the headmaster and my class teacher insisted that I could do it. The topic given to me was Salt Satyagraha and I had to speak on it for 15 minutes. My father helped me prepare the speech.

But, on the day of the speech, I was very tense. The only consolation was that except for one student, who was smart and could speak well, the others were in the same boat as me.

I went on the stage when my name was called. I was nervous, and my eyesight blurred on seeing such a large audience. I fumbled on the first few words, but then surprisingly, I composed myself and delivered the speech flawlessly. The headmaster and my other teachers were pleasantly surprised and gave me the second prize. Since that day, I gained the confidence to speak on public platforms.

I was considered a reasonably good student. In the SSLC exam in 1956, I stood second among 70 students. I missed the first rank by just three marks, which I regretted; I felt later that I should have worked a little harder. Incidentally, I was the youngest student to clear the SSLC exam at the age of 14 years.

Next on the agenda was joining Intermediate classes (Standard XII-XIII). My father wanted me to study at Rajahmundry Government Arts College. The zamindar of Kapileswarapuram, who was close to my father, had guest houses in Rajahmundry. He suggested that I stay in their guest house and pursue my studies there. The city was also very close to our village. But my maternal uncle, who was a doctor and the father-in-law of my elder brother, was upset with my father's decision and sent word that I must be immediately brought to Kakinada, where he lived. He arranged for my admission in the Intermediate class (math, physics, chemistry or MPC) at Pithapur Raja's (PR) Government

College. My father could not say no; I joined the college in June 1956.

I faced two major problems after shifting to Kakinada. It was my first time away from home, so I was homesick, even though my uncle and aunt treated me very well and my sister-inlaw also looked after me. Soon after, my father visited us for 10 days as he had party work in Kakinada, which was the district Congress headquarters. Besides, during Dassara and Sankranti, we had holidays for 15 days each, and I used to count the days until the time I would visit home. I eventually settled in.

The second problem was language. Up to the SSLC, I had studied in a Telugu-medium school. English was just one of the subjects. Luckily, it did not take me very long to get used to being instructed in the English medium. The other subjects are English and Telugu literature.

Our class was big, comprising 110 students. Not everyone was serious about studies. I was very serious and attentive in class. I remember an incident that left my classmates in awe of me. DSR, the Algebra lecturer derived the Binomial Theorem, which was quite long, on the blackboard. After that, he challenged whether any of us can repeat it. After some hesitation, I stood up. Everyone was surprised as I was considered a shy boy. I repeated the entire theorem without any mistakes. DSR complimented me profusely. Some of my classmates couldn't believe I just picked it up then; some of them said I must have practised the theorem at home, but I hadn't.

Our classes were conducted at two places. The maths, physics, and chemistry classes were held in a building adjoining PR College High School because the laboratories were located there. English and Telugu classes were held in the main building, which was situated on a large campus with a playground, a little distance away. Most of the students were from either PR High School or from other local schools. Only a few of us were from outside Kakinada. But everyone got along well. A few girl students were also there, but they would sit separately in a group.

My Intermediate classes went on smoothly. Apart from classes, we had sports, games, social science sessions, drama and music competitions, and picnics. I participated in sports and games and had volunteered for the social science sessions. Once, when I participated in an agitation against a major shopping complex, my uncle came to know about it and gave me a dressing down. After that, I never participated in such protests.

In the final examination, I got reasonably good marks, but they were not good enough to get admission in the mechanical engineering course at the local college. I might have been able to get admission in other subjects at some far-off colleges, but I was not interested in going and living so far, and neither was my father.

So, I joined the BA course at PR College with mathematics as my main subject. All the classes were held in the main building. It was a two-year course and I was doing very well. In fact, I was pretty popular. Interestingly, I was doing well in the languages too, particularly in English and Telugu poetry.

I passed B.A. with great distinction. I secured 99.8% in maths and 100% in algebra, trigonometry, calculus, analytical geometry, statics, dynamics, and hydrostatics. I secured a little less than 100% in statistics. I was happy and so was my family. I received my B.A. degree in June 1960.

My problems started when I told my uncle, who was a PH.D in Economics from USA and Director of NCAER, that I wanted to do my post-graduation and doctoral degree in mathematics and become a professor at a university. He had other plans for me. He wanted me to go to the US and pursue my studies and career there in economics, with specialisation in econometrics. It would pay me back in the long term, he felt. My elder brother supported him as everyone was enamoured with the idea of studying and living abroad. My uncle said that in this case, I need not do my post-graduation. A one-year certificate course in economics at any college would suffice. My brother used his contacts to get me informally admitted to Amalapuram College and I started attending final year BA economics classes there. Many of my new classmates wondered why I had demoted myself after getting a first class in maths.

Unfortunately, I could not continue my studies. After three months, I was struck with typhoid. I returned to my parents' home where the doctor suggested that I be taken to Kakinada immediately. My father did so, but even after many days of treatment, the fever would not come down. In fact, it worsened, and I went into a comma. Among the doctors looking after me was the superintendent of the district general hospital. He arranged for a medicine which had come to the market recently and said it may be my last chance. Luckily, the medicine worked, and my fever came down. Soon, I was back to almost normal. And went back home. However, after a week, the fever relapsed. We again went to my uncle's house in Kakinada for treatment. After one more month, I was fully cured of the disease.

Once the academic year was over, the matter of my further studies came up again. My uncle and my brother decided, and I also agreed that I would do my post-graduation in statistics. Accordingly, I joined M.A. (statistics) at Karnataka University, Dharwad, in June 1961. The university campus was beautiful. It is situated on the Chota Mahabaleshwar hill. The climate was good too. The university is housed in a massive building that could be seen from a distance. The statistics department was on the second floor and the library was on the ground floor. I stayed at the university hostel, which was nearby. In the first year, I stayed in a double room with one of my classmates. In the second year, I shifted to a single room.

Apart from lectures, we attended practical classes where statistical parameters were calculated, and conclusions were drawn. There were no computers or calculators. Facit machines were available. We also attended seminars and special lectures by outside speakers. In the first year, four common subjects were taught to all students. We were a class of 20 and had a professor, a reader, two lecturers, a demonstrator, and an office assistant.

In the second year, we had two common subjects and two special papers. My specialisation was sampling theory, which was taught by the professor. The other subjects that I took were stochastic process and design of experiments, taught by a reader. I did well in the two subjects, both in the practicals and in the seminar, and stood second in class in the final exam with a first class.

Life on the university campus was good. The vice-chancellor (DC Pavate) was very popular and would regularly inquire about our welfare, teaching, etc. The food was good; chapatis, bajra, and jowar rotis were the staples. There was a good canteen for breakfast and evening snacks. Lunch and dinner were served in the hostel and the expenses shared on a cooperative basis.

I picked up working knowledge of Kannada. Sports and games facilities were also available. Inspired by one of my classmates, I developed an interest in yoga. We used to practise yoga in a small, remote forest and I became reasonably good at the practice. I was interested in the Student Congress and hostel committee activities, but as advised by my father, I didn't get involved too deeply.

We had two excursions. One was to Goa, soon after its liberation from Portuguese rule. Goa was very beautiful, neat, and clean, with many beaches and temples and churches. The other was a visit to Mysore (now Mysuru) and Bangalore (now Bengaluru). A few of us visited Hampi Vijayanagar also. While in University, we made an interesting observation—every student would say that he/she was doing M.Sc. and not M.A. We realised that to say one was doing M.A. was embarrassing as it sounds like the Kannada word for buffalo (emme).

After the exams were over and holidays were declared, I went home like most other students. Before leaving, I had a chat with my professor about my future and joining the Ph.D. programme. He promised to support me. Of course, there would be a formal application process and I would also have to try to get a University Grants Commission (UGC) scholarship. But that was not to be.

I enjoyed my holidays at home. But, soon there was some discord over my future studies. My Uncle and brother decided that I should join Delhi School of Economics in the M.A. Economics & Statistics course. I did not like the idea of joining a course which can be done after B.A. But my Uncle insisted that it will help get admission in a U.S. University. Reluctantly, I joined, but it did not work out and I had to discontinue, return home and valuable time was lost.

After returning from Delhi, I concentrated on looking for a job. Accordingly, I started preparing for bank recruitment exams, lecturer posts' exams, the All India Services Examinations, etc.

I got a couple offers for a lecturer's post, but they were mostly in junior colleges. Finally, I found a good job as a lecturer of mathematics and statistics at Jawaharlal Nehru Krishi Vishwavidyalaya, Jabalpur; I was posted at the Sehore campus in Madhya Pradesh. Later, I got a job in the statistics department of the Reserve Bank of India (RBI) in *Bombay* (now Mumbai). After working for a few months, I again started thinking of further studies. There were a couple of options in front of me. Most bankers who were interested in improving their career path pursued a course at the Certified Associate of India Institute of Bankers (CAIIB). It was a somewhat leisurely activity that could be done simultaneously with other courses as many subjects were common. Some also managed to get an L.L.B. degree by joining evening classes. The second option was to pursue a Ph.D. in statistics at Karnataka University. The third option was to try to get admission in the statistics department of a US university.

I explored about the last option first. It wouldn't be so difficult for me to get admission given my good academic record and recommendations from my Karnataka University professors, one of whom was from a US university himself. But getting an assistantship or a scholarship would be very difficult, particularly after the India-Pakistan War of 1965.

Compared to that, doing a Ph.D. in statistics at Bombay University would be relatively easier. Karnataka University was recognised by

Bombay University as it was part of the Bombay presidency before the reorganisation of the Indian states, and their syllabi were mostly the same. I met the head of the department and he said he could help me, but the only problem was there was no guide readily available in the field of my specialization. I could change the subject, but that would take some time. Also, as it was a highly specialised field, future opportunities wouldn't be great. Finally, I decided to do my Ph.D. in economics.

I met Professor R. Bharadwaj, the head of the department of economics at Bombay University, at his office in the Fort area of the city, close to my office. He listened to me patiently and readily agreed to be my guide. But as I was in a full-time job, doing regular classes at the university would be impossible. There was also the option of doing an M.A. in economics through research, i.e. by submitting a substantial dissertation. The professor suggested I work on that.

Accordingly, I registered myself at the university with him as my guide. He was a specialist in econometrics and input-output analysis. After going through extensive writings in input-output analysis and general economics, I suggested two topics to him for my thesis. He agreed on one—'Structural Inter-linkages between Public and Private Sectors in the Indian Industry'. I had to work really hard, going through research on the subject, attending seminars, conferences, classes that I found interesting, interacting with the professors, etc. On Sundays and other holidays, when everyone else was relaxing, I would visit the university library and study.

I would also attend annual econometric and input-output analysis conferences, taking leave from work and spending my own money. All the hard work paid off finally when I submitted the thesis. Thereafter, registering for the Ph.D. became easy. I suggested considering a macro-econometric model for the Indian economy emphasising on six sectors—agriculture, industry, price, money, foreign trade, banking, and national income. Professor Bharadwaj provisionally agreed to this. But, just as I started working on the project, he had to leave on a foreign assignment for two years. He suggested that I pursue my work and that he would clear it after his return.

In the meantime, Professor P.R. Brahmanand, a renowned professor and author of many books, became the head of the department of economics at the university. During one of my library visits, I met him and had a long discussion with him. He asked me to meet him again. In the second or third meeting, he suggested that I change my subject and construct an econometric model of his pet theory of a wage goods model. I did not have much knowledge on the subject. However, I couldn't say no to him as he was a very senior and respected academician.

I read all the available research on the topic and many books authored by him. Then I prepared a draft synopsis of my thesis. He made a few suggestions. I had to put in a lot of work as I had to create a host of date series on wage goods and related areas. Anyway, my thesis, entitled 'The Macro-Economic Process in India—A New Classical Exploration' finally took shape and I submitted the draft to him. He was extremely busy and took some time to clear it. When Bombay University decided to confirm my Ph.D., I was elated. There were many twists and turns in my education, but in the end, I achieved my goal.

Rising through the ranks / A job well done

ೞ

My search for a job started from Atreyapuram. I was preparing for the All India Services, national financial institutions' exams, and responding to advertisements for lecturers' jobs in reputed Indian institutions, among others. I had also registered my name at the employment exchange. One of my seniors at Karnataka University, whose career had suffered because he took up a low-profile job, advised me not to make the same mistake. So, I turned down an offer for a junior college lecturer's post and a statistician's job in two different industries. If I was not clear about the job profile and future prospects, I wouldn't attend the interview.

Finally, I got a job of my liking as a lecturer of mathematics and statistics at the Jawaharlal Nehru Krishi Vishwa Vidyalaya (JNKVV), headquartered in Jabalpur, Madhya Pradesh. I was posted at their Sehore campus, near Bhopal. I went there by train. Sehore is a district headquarters town and the state capital, Bhopal, is in the same district. But there were no hotels in Sehore; only dharamshalas. I was hesitant to stay at one, but a rickshawpuller I met there assured me they were good. The first person I met in Sehore was the district education officer. I also met a few state government officers who were staying at the same dharamshala as me. Their polite and reassuring words gave me some confidence about the place.

I reported to the principal of Rafi Kidwai Agricultural College under the JNKVV, where I was supposed to work. I shifted to a big room in the hostel complex where food and snacks were available at low, subsidised rates. I had a detailed discussion with the principal about my job responsibilities. My main job was to give lectures to the postgraduate students in statistical subjects, particularly in the Design of Experiments (DOE) stream.

Secondly, I had to assist students in their dissertations where the statistical tools of DOE were applied. The main purpose of this was to suggest the optimum use of fertilisers and other inputs to maximise crop yield. The main crops in the region were wheat, potato, tomatoes, and pulses. My work went on very well and I could see that I was a big help to the students who hadn't mastered statistical techniques. I would also consult with other lecturers on the concerned topics. All my students' dissertations were accepted by the university committee. I also took a few math classes for degree students. The university followed the trimester system. I was the youngest lecturer there, but everyone, including the principal, treated me with utmost respect.

There wasn't much by way of social life in Sehore. There was only one cinema theatre. It was owned by the father of one of the students, so we got free tickets. The college was situated on the outskirts of the city and commuting was difficult. I was planning to buy a cycle, but the principal suggested that I use one of the spare cycles on the campus. In my leisure time, I used to read research papers and statistical subjects, besides books on economics, to keep myself abreast of things. I was also preparing for the competitive exams on the side.

One day, the principal called me and informed me that there were transfer orders to shift me to the Raipur campus. The lecturer at Raipur was a native of Sehore and he had requested for a transfer there. The principal told me that he would miss me as I had become popular among the students. However, I did not feel too bad about leaving, as by that time, I had appeared for a written test for a position in the statistics department of the Reserve Bank of India (RBI). I had done the test well and was expecting an interview call and possible selection for the post.

I reported to the principal of the Raipur campus; the quarters on the campus had already been allotted. The only problem was that I would have to cook my own meals. The lecturer in plant pathology was also a bachelor and we became friends. The lecturer in English and Hindi was originally from Andhra Pradesh, but his parents were now settled in Raipur. We would go to his house, where he lived with his uncle, and eat tasty snacks there. The college had a spare cycle and I would use it to go to the city.

My job here was simple—I just had to teach. I got a chance to attend some academic meetings on the Indore and Jabalpur campuses of the college. There were more visits to Jabalpur as it was the university headquarters. The meetings were mainly to exchange news and views about the developments on each campus, making changes in course content wherever necessary, and holding seminars and conferences.

As expected, I received an interview call from RBI and was selected for the post. I resigned from the JNKVV and joined RBI in August 1965. The principal was quite unhappy to lose my services as I was doing very well.

When I first moved to Bombay, I stayed at a hotel that was near the VT station, which was also close to the RBI building. I reported for duty and was posted in the Flow of Funds division. I was briefed about my work, which was very different from my previous roles. It took me some time to adjust to the 10:00 to 6:00 desk job. A lecturer's job was obviously more comfortable.

The Flow of Funds division prepares annual statements on financial flows in the Indian economy. The economy is divided into 12 sectors and a matrix of flows among them is prepared. I asked for some reference material on the topic to work on my study and was asked to use the office library, which was in the same building. I borrowed some books from there and devoted a lot of time to understanding the topic. I would also talk to my experienced colleagues and bosses and ask them questions. In due course, the study was published in the RBI monthly bulletin. My bosses were impressed by my performance and complimented me. The study gave me an insight into the interdependence of various financial sectors.

This study was an annual feature, on the basis of which some special reports were prepared for the top management. I was also deputed for hands-on training in the 'Economic classification of central and state government budgets' in the ministry of finance, Government of India, New Delhi.

Next, I was posted to the company's finance division. In this division, the balance sheets of companies were analysed, summarised, interpreted, and brought out as an annual study. There were separate studies carried out for large and small companies and foreign-controlled rupee companies. All the studies were published in the RBI monthly bulletin. Basically, they were accounting analyses and interpretations arrived at through various ratios. It was a new subject for me and so I had to learn a lot here as well. Soon, I had a good understanding of the subject.

I also made some gains thanks to my then boss, who took a keen interest in the share market. The balance sheet analysis helped him choose the right companies to invest in. A simple man, he not only made money himself but also introduced us to share trading. But, I'd always been warned that share market trading was akin to gambling and that one could lose huge amounts of money. However, due to my boss's constant encouragement, I started investing in shares in a small way. I made some money for additional expenses. Later, the knack for share trading helped me make a fair bit of money.

Next, I was posted in the electronic data processing division of RBI. I got some programming training there and was given the job of processing banking statistics. There wasn't much programme development to do. Our computer system was installed at the Bhabha Atomic Research Centre (BARC), Trombay, for security reasons. The computer would work round the clock, and we had to work in eight-hour shifts. I used to prefer the morning shift (7:00 am to 3:00 pm) or the night shift as they allowed me time to go to Bombay University to meet my professors, attend seminars and conferences, and do library work. After the bank nationalisation, there was a huge demand for generations of statements based on data. I would deliver the required statements fast and this was well-appreciated by the top management. The data was also useful in carrying out studies, some of which were published in the RBI Bulletin.

My next posting was in the econometrics division. By that time, my M.A. (economics) work was over. This work was in my field of specialisation. The RBI had developed a macroeconometric model for key sectors. My job was tracking money and the banking, fiscal, and foreign trade sectors. Immediately after the Union Budget presentation, which was at 5:00 PM in those days, I would feed the model with new data and it would arrive at projections of critical parameters like savings, deposit growth, inflation, and national income. The results had to reach the top management by midnight. It was a challenging job, but I did it well and received appreciation.

Another task that put me in the spotlight and brought me accolades was the Sixth Five Year Plan estimates. A committee was appointed under the chairmanship of one of the deputy governors to project the financial savings for various sectors during the plan period. My boss was a member of the committee and I was assisting him. The project was time-bound.

Once, my boss fell sick just ahead of an important meeting in the RBI main building. As he was not there, I did not go to the meeting. I received a phone call and was admonished for not turning up and was ordered to come immediately. Luckily, all the calculations and draft notes were ready. The results, including calculations made by me, were discussed. I was also advised that it was a time-bound programme and I should be working on a war-footing even in my boss's absence.

A senior executive gave me an analogy: when an actual war is on, if the commander is immobilised for any reason, the next in command automatically takes charge without waiting for orders from the headquarters. I got the message loud and clear and became a regular participant in the meetings. It was an excellent experience and training to shoulder bigger responsibilities. The meetings were attended by senior executives from the Planning

Commission, the Central Statistics Office (CSO) and the Finance Ministry, apart from RBI officials.

I also had the privilege of publishing three studies in RBI's occasional papers and attended econometrics and economics seminars, apart from the Input-Output Research Association's annual conferences. I was also selected to attend a computer programme at the Indian Statistical Institute (ISI), Calcutta (now known as Kolkata). Many institutions invited me as a guest faculty. Soon, I was recognised and selected as a direct recruit for the position of a research officer by RBI. I had a very fruitful and satisfactory stint at RBI. It greatly helped me in my academic pursuits as well as my career growth.

In 1982, I beat stiff competition to be selected as a deputy general manager (economist) at the Industrial Development Bank of India (IDBI), which was initially a wholly owned organisation of RBI and later became a central government owned corporation. I joined IDBI in October that year.

The first task assigned to me by my boss, the Economic Advisor, was to plan and bring out a comprehensive study on the financial performance of IDBI-assisted companies. My boss gave me some instructions and told me that the contents of the study had to be in line with the needs of the bank. I first interacted with the project appraisal department to understand what factors they considered while sanctioning loans. Next, I met the follow-up teams. I then drew up the important balance sheet items required on both the liability and asset sides. I also studied the various ratios needed.

Finally, I submitted a draft of the study. My boss and his experienced colleagues made some suggestions. Three officers were assigned to me to carry out the analysis for the project. I made them undergo some informal training under my erstwhile colleagues at RBI. Finally, the draft study was ready, based on the data of 650-700 IDBI-assisted companies.

Soon after, the draft was cleared and published. It got favourable responses from IDBI chairman, the press, finance ministry officials, and other intellectuals. My boss, of course, complimented me. The publication continued for a number of years even after I left the department. It was very useful for project finance, rehabilitation finance, and the department itself, apart from government and private Institutions.

My other responsibilities were carrying out studies on various topics, preparing notes for internal use, attending to the finance ministry's requirements, conducting academic studies, attending conferences, fielding parliamentary queries and organising induction courses for newly recruited officers. I would also have to interact with officials from the International Monetary Fund (IMF), the World Bank, the Asian Development Bank (ADB), other institutions, and so on.

I also had to carry out econometric and other studies when presentations were made in IDBI. Once, the chairman called me and said that there was a presentation by a specialist of an international organization. The presentation is expected to be highly technical using mathematical methods and I had to take care of it by proper observations and comments. I quickly brushed up on my knowledge on difference and differential equations, which I had studied long ago. I had a clear understanding of the econometric technique and model part. As luck would have it, I managed to catch three crucial flaws in the logic and assumptions put forth in the presentation. The scholars accepted my points and promised to rectify them. The chairman called me to his chamber and thanked me profusely for showing the bank in good light.

On another occasion, I received a message that the chairman wanted to see me immediately. I went to him, a bit tense. Our Executive Director was also sitting with him. I thought I would be rebuked for some lapse I had committed. But it turned out to be a pleasant surprise. The Government of India wanted to start a development bank for the northeast. I was to prepare a draft constitution of various activities. I returned to my cabin, called a bright young officer who was well-versed in computers. Both of us went through articles of association of development bank, state financial and industrial development bank and pencilmarked areas that were important. The officer quickly prepared a draft on his computer and it was duly put up for approval by the evening. The chairman made some changes to it and got it vetted by the legal department. He thanked us for our good work.

At one point, IDBI merged technical and financial officers and economists into one common stream, which was governed by what was known as common seniority. I was transferred to the operational department of project finance. The work involved receiving project loan applications and appraising them on five parameters—management, market, technical, economic, and commercial factors. Once all the parameters were met, the project would be recommended for sanction. I was in charge of new projects in the electronic, power, and cement industries. I was assisted by three technical officers. Some of the applications were very new-age—like software technology parks, gas-based combined cycle power project. We sanctioned three projects in this area. World bank sanctioned a line of credit to modernize the cement industry. We sanctioned loans to quite a few cement projects jointly with other DFIs. Before starting the appraisal process, we used to get a briefing from competent external specialists in the field. I spent a very successful and satisfactory two years in the department.

I was assigned the task to establish an EDP division in IDBI.

I successfully completed this with the help of a consultant including selection of computers, getting them installed, recruitment of manpower, and training in a short time.

After this, I was transferred to our Ahmedabad branch. It covered operations across Gujarat. The main business was providing refinance to small and medium industrial units, which were assisted by state-level financial institutions and commercial banks. I was a director on the boards of both the state financial corporation and the state industrial investment corporation. The board members comprised of some eminent industrialists and senior IAS officers. My critical comments and suggestions for modifications and improvements were given due importance by the boards. When IDBI introduced new schemes like asset credit, equipment finance, and special loans, I was very cautious as in some cases, people would try to get finance twice.

I had cordial relations with all industrialists, industry associations, and voluntary agencies. I was a regular invitee to seminars on venture capital finance and IDBI schemes. I was invited as a chief guest and a guest speaker at many forums. In a couple of events where small-scale industrialists were the main audience, I was requested to speak in Hindi. I obliged even though I couldn't speak the language very well. The speeches were well-received. I was satisfied as IDBI's business in Gujarat increased by more than 50% during my tenure.

In June 1992, I was transferred to the Eastern regional office, Calcutta. It was totally different from Ahmedabad both in terms of the business and the environment. West Bengal, Bihar, and Orissa were under our jurisdiction. Project finance, refinance, administration, and the personnel departments were under my charge. The sanction of loans improved even though some factories were located elsewhere while their offices were in Calcutta. I had to appraise two projects in Bihar in Hindi as the promoters were not comfortable with English. All the people were nice and courteous. Some of the West Bengal ministers were very well-educated and sophisticated in their interactions with us. In Calcutta too, business picked up substantially after I joined.

One time, I had to face a workers' agitation at a steel plant which had been closed due to social unrest. The workers' union leaders insisted that IDBI pay their salaries. Around 300-400 workers along with their leaders encircled our office building, shouting slogans. My boss, who was the chief general manager, had gone on leave. A bit unsure how to handle the situation, I got in touch with the state industries minister for advice. He asked me not to worry and told me I should listen to the workers carefully without provoking them. He also asked me to assure them that I would convey their demands to our head office. I listened to the leaders of four-five workers' unions patiently and assured them that I would convey their feelings to our chairman. The meeting went off smoothly.

On another occasion, our own employee unions were agitating for the removal of the bank's doctor and demanding a new one. I spoke to our head office in their presence. They left my cabin before 8:00 PM as, otherwise, they could have been arrested under the law. Both the union leaders were very respectful towards me.

I had to tour all the three states—West Bengal, Bihar, and Orissa—for business canvassing, seminars, industry meetings, etc. My tenure in Calcutta (Kolkata) was interesting and satisfying.

After this, I was transferred back to the head office in Mumbai and posted in my parent department, the Research and Planning Department (RPD). After a couple of months, I received a phone call at my residence from the Executive Director personnel department. He requested me to take charge of our training institute, the Jawaharlal Nehru Institute for Development Banking (JNIDB), in Hyderabad. I asked him for how long my services would be required there. He said the tenure was likely to be short. I agreed without even enquiring the reason for the short tenure. My mother, brother, and two sisters lived in Hyderabad and I was happy that I would be able to spend some time with them.

After reporting to Hyderabad, I came to know what he meant. The workers employed by the JNIDB contractors had been protesting for a long time and this had disrupted the training programmes. The management thought a person who knew the local language would be useful in such a situation. Also, I had the experience of handling agitations in Calcutta.

Anyway, I took the matter in my hands and decided to resolve it. I informally contacted many politicians, including ministers, and some industrialists. The protest was being led by a politician. I consulted all the contractors who were providing us technical workers and labourers. Finally, I got through to the persons behind the stir. One was an MP and another was a local legislator and union leader. I spoke with them and settled the matter by agreeing to hire some more employees. The contractors readily agreed to this. The district superintendent of police helped me a lot in resolving the matter, as did one of our officers. I thought my job there was over, but the management asked me to continue working in Hyderabad.

The JNIDB was an international training institute for executives of the Association of Development Financing Institutions (ADFIAP), particularly from SAARC countries. A number of programmes were conducted there, of which a course on appraising power projects, conducted by Harvard University faculty, is worth mentioning. The programme got an overwhelming response and was even attended by some IAS officers. We had a computer lab where the actual appraisal was done by trainees. The course was so popular it was conducted a second time.

We had specially designed programmes for ADFIAP member institutions. There was another programme for state financial institutes. Exclusive courses were conducted for the officers of the development banks of Mauritius and Sri Lanka. We also had some regular programmes on project appraisal and follow-up etc. My assignment in Hyderabad was hectic and satisfying. I was transferred back to the head office in Bombay after two years.

This time, I was appointed as Chief General Manager (CGM) and head of the RPD, which I had left as DGM. My responsibilities included a wide range of activities encompassing all the functions of IDBI. I was heading the departments of economic research, budget and planning, associate institutions, and press and public relations. My other responsibilities included serving in various internal committees like the senior executive, asset liability management, resource, and risk assessing committees. I also had to liaise with the RBI, the Finance Ministry, the World Bank, the ADB, and rating agencies, both international and domestic.

I also had to look after the arrangements for the visits of parliamentary committees on various industries. Preparing replies to parliamentary queries, attending meetings of international institutions on behalf of IDBI, and attending board and managing committee meetings whenever required were also part of my job. Another important responsibility I had was preparing estimates and getting approvals for quarterly, half-yearly and annual budgets for the bank's operations. I was also responsible for preparing the draft annual report for the approval of the board of directors. In short, my presence was required in almost all the activities of the bank. I had to travel frequently to attend government meetings. My tenure as CGM was very busy and enjoyable.

IDBI appoints its executives to the board of assisted companies as directors to keep a watchful eye on the implementation of projects, optimal spending of resources, delay and diversion of funds, cost and time overruns, and to bring projects into production. The nominee directors have to send periodic reports to the management. I had the privilege of working as a nominee director in 15-20 companies. I served the bank till the age of 66 as its nominee.

I also served on the Advisory Committee of economic research institutions like the National Council of Applied Economic Research, the Indian Council for Research on International Economic Relations, etc, to whom IDBI had given grants.

I attended some international training programs and represented IDBI at many international seminars, meetings, and conferences. I attended a two-week programme on Finance and Control conducted by the International Institute for Management Development (IMD) in Lausanne, Switzerland. I attended a four-week Trainers Training Programme at RIPA International, London. I was deputed for a conference on Managing the Global Economy in the Light of Asian Crises in London. I attended the 65th annual celebrations of the Mexican Development Bank and made a presentation on financing the SME sector in India.

I was deputed to attend an international seminar on development banking organised by the Development Bank of Columbia in Kartagina. I attended the World Economic Forum meeting held in Melbourne, Australia, from September 11th 13th, 2000. I also participated in the 73rd Industrial Finance Seminar held from March 5th-10th, 2001 in Tokyo, organised by the Industrial Bank of Japan. On my way back, I met officials of the Development Bank of Singapore for a possible collaboration for transforming into a universal bank. I had meetings with officials of the European Central Bank, Deutsche Bank, and Commerzbank in Frankfurt. My last foreign assignment was holding meetings with officials of the Nepal Development Bank for a possible tie-up that they wanted.

I had a challenging, fruitful, and enjoyable tenure at IDBI and retired as Executive Director and Economic Advisor on May 31st, 2002, after nearly 40 years of active service.

The wedding people talked about for ages

ॐ

My marriage was an interesting affair and it was a topic of discussion among my family members and relatives for many years after. Even though I was shy and somewhat reserved, most of my relatives liked me as I was considered an obedient son, a good student, and an intelligent person. Besides, I did not have any bad habits and did not interfere in other people's matters. To add to this, I had a good post-graduate degree with a job at a prestigious national institution.

There was a shortage of good prospective bridegrooms in our village. So, even though we were not very rich, many people wanted to offer their daughters' hands to me in marriage. At one time, there were eight persons who considered me as a prospective son-in-law, waiting for the time my father decided to arrange my marriage.

On one of my visits home, my mother brought up the topic of my marriage. I told her that any girl from our village would find it difficult to adjust in a big city like Bombay where the language and culture were totally different. It would be better if I married a girl from Bombay, preferably someone who was employed and could supplement my income. My mother probably thought that I had some girl in mind and conveyed this to my father with a request to expedite my nuptials.

Two events further added a sense of urgency to the matter. One, the Godavari Pushkaram (Kumbh Mela) was starting in a few months' time, and there would be no muhurtham (auspicious date) for one entire year. Second, since I had unsuccessfully tried to go to the US for higher studies, my father thought that I may still want to go abroad. This spelt potential danger of me marrying an

American girl. They cited examples of a close friend of my father, who was with him in the freedom movement. He had sent his son to the US amid great fanfare, but the boy ended up marrying an American girl and, in due course, was totally separated from his roots.

My father, therefore, decided to put my marriage on a fast track. He faced some quick disappointments while hunting for a bride for me. Some wedding agents would paint an exaggerated picture of the girl and her family and they would turn out to be nothing like that. Meanwhile, my mother had a sweet spot for two girls who were from her brothers' families, but my father rejected them. Thus, the bride hunting process had become burdensome for my parents.

Just when my father had decided that he would no longer encourage people who did not look dependable prima facie, a man approached him, offering his niece's hand in marriage for me. He had great respect for my father and was also a distant relative of ours. When he requested my father to come and see Bhanumathi Devi, he readily agreed. Once he saw her, he gave his approval for our marriage.

The bride's father and his mother-in-law discussed the terms and conditions in detail with my father; he agreed to most of them. A muhurtham was set for the wedding. But, the bride's side suggested that it would be better if the bride and groom saw each other. My father said it was not necessary, but the girl's uncle said that since the bridegroom was well-behaved and doing a good job, there was no cause for worry.

Later, I came to know that the bride's father, who worked in the central excise and customs department, had made some inquiries about me at my place of work. The brother of one of his colleagues was an executive in RBI in the same department. This person gave positive report about me and the girl's family was satisfied.

My father told me that the wedding had been finalised and the muhurtham was fixed. I had to plan my trip home accordingly. I was sent a photograph of the girl. I could see from the picture that she was not only very young (about 16) but also a typical village girl. I was worried how she would adjust in Bombay. She had just done her pre-university course (PUC) in Guntur, where her father was working. The age difference also was significant.

I decided to ask my father to call off the wedding. That day, after work, I was walking to VT station to board a local train to go home. It is a straight road known as Bazargate Street. As I was crossing the road to get to the station, I changed my mind. After all, my father was my well-wisher, and he would not do anything that wasn't in my interest. I didn't want to hurt him by rejecting his choice. I entered the GPO, which was near the station, and sent him a telegram accepting his proposal.

The wedding was barely 10 days away. I had to get some wedding cards printed and invite some of my friends and colleagues to the event. But I did not know the bride's name. I got it in the reply telegram my father sent me.

My wedding was fixed for April 26th, 1967, Wednesday, at 7:35 PM. As per the Telugu calendar, it was plavanga nama samvatsara, chaitra masa, bahula paksha, vidiya.

I decided to give the first wedding invite to the statistical advisor of RBI. He was from our district. His elder brother and my father had been close during the freedom struggle. After receiving the card, he asked me whether I had seen the bride. When I said no, he laughed aloud and asked me whether I had given my father all the authority over my life. He then conveyed his best wishes for a happy married life.

I did not have any leave left, but the bank was kind enough to grant me a week of leave. In those days, there were no direct trains from Bombay V.T. station to Rajahmundry. I had to change trains in Hyderabad. By the time I reached Atreyapuram, there was no time for the 'grooming' rituals. The wedding was to take place in Attili, a village in the neighbouring district. But we had to cross the Vasishta river as well as the bridge at Siddantham village and had to leave immediately.

In those days, marriage parties comprising family and friends of the bridegroom would hire buses on contract and all the guests would travel to the wedding destination together, amid much fun and fanfare. We too went to Attili by bus. The bride's family had arranged a Vididhi, a guest house, for the marriage party to stay in. We got off the bus and were waiting as the servants unloaded the luggage when a gentleman approached my father and welcomed us. There were some other people with him as well.

Then he started walking around, seemingly looking for someone. When he did not find the person he was looking for, he looked worried. He came back to my father and hesitatingly asked him whether the bridegroom hadn't come with them. My father laughed loudly and said yes, he had.

The man, my would-be father-in-law, couldn't identify me as I didn't have the signs of a bridegroom. Due to my late arrival, I had no time to wear new clothes, paint kumkum crosses on my feet, and wear a tilak on my forehead. Besides, there were at least half-a-dozen men in the wedding party in my age group. My father called out to me and introduced me to him. His face was visibly relieved. He enquired whether I wanted to see the bride. I said no, as it would serve no purpose at that stage. My elder brother and sisters went to see her.

The next morning, the rituals started. There were separate rituals and functions for the bride and for me. In the evening, the wedding proceedings started. That was the first time I saw my would-be wife. I was happy.

In our community, as in most others, marriage functions are a time for enjoyment marked by religious ceremonies, families and friends meeting and hanging out, fun and laughter, sumptuous feasts, and exchanging of gifts, mostly dresses, gold and silver jewellery, and household articles. For dinner, apart from the marriage parties from both the sides, villagers were also invited. There is usually a set menu for weddings, comprising sweets, savouries, and main courses. One of the special items served at my wedding was kaja, a sweetmeat made of maida, sugar syrup, and some flavouring.

At Andhra weddings, the groom's party takes a special pleasure in teasing the bride's party. Our party decided to gorge on the sweets, which they assessed were in limited supply, until they were finished. Our priest was also a member of the party. Soon, the kajas were in short supply.

My father-in-law and others from the bride's side got worried and came and spoke to my father, as shortage of food is taken as an affront by the groom's family, and might even result in the groom's party walking out of the wedding. My father, smiling to himself, assured them that nothing of the sort would happen and asked them to join in the fun as well. The wedding went off peacefully. It was such a memorable event that it was a talking point among our friends and relatives for many years. Later, they were even more impressed that we had a successful and happy marriage despite not having seen each other before the wedding.

We all returned to Atreyapuram along with the bride and I spent a couple of days at my parents' home. Some functions were organised to introduce the new bride to the entire village. I was to return to Bombay alone for now while she stayed with my parents.

After a couple of months, I went back to the village and then to my in-laws' place to bring my wife to Bombay. We came to Hyderabad first and took a train to Bombay. The train doesn't stop at Thane, where I lived, so we got down at Kalyan and boarded a local train to Thane. It was my wife's first long distance train journey. The train was very crowded, so some of my friends helped us board and get off.

My wife was well received in my residential colony by an elderly lady. Other Telugu-speaking ladies also came and spoke to her. So, initial apprehensions were laid to rest. She interacted with everyone and soon picked up some Hindi too. She was liked by all for her simplicity, friendliness, and her hospitality.

Our neighbours empathised with her as she was very young, so much so that I would be chided if they felt I was ignoring her. One day, I came home late at night from a seminar at the university. One of our neighbours rebuked me for coming home so late and leaving her alone at home. The initial problems over, she adjusted to her new world very well.

Full house

ಬಾ

After about six months in Thane, we moved to a new house in Ghatkopar. The complex we lived in comprised six buildings belonging to RBI employees' societies. So, many of the residents in the area were already known to me; some of them were even from my own department.

We started socialising with them and would often invite them to our house. We had good neighbours here as well. My wife made her own women friends whom she would call over for a cup of tea sometimes. Of course, most of her friends were Telugu-speaking. Slowly, as she picked up Hindi, she made friends with people from other communities as well. My wife was also a good host and would offer tea, coffee and snacks to our guests. Festivals and social functions also accorded us opportunities to meet new people.

We had settled in by now and I realised that my worries that my wife would be lonely and homesick were unfounded. We had a smooth and happy married life. The atmosphere at my workplace was also congenial, and I had a number of close friends there.

After some time, I noticed that my wife wasn't keeping well. Many a time, I stepped in to do the cooking. I was a good cook and enjoyed it. Worried about her health, I took her to our family doctor. It turned out that she was expecting. The doctor congratulated us and gave us tips on how she could maintain good health during this time.

Happy to hear the good news, I conveyed the same to my parents and in-laws. They too were very happy. But, at the same time, we were all a bit worried as she was still young, and nobody was in a position to come and assist us. My mother was old and had to look after my father. My mother-in-law had her own young children and her old mother to look after. Besides, my father-in-law was in a transferable job and had to shift base every two years. So, there was nobody to come and assist us during the delivery if it were to be scheduled at Bombay. The only option was to send her to her parents' place for the delivery.

Meanwhile, I had to take on multiple roles to get things moving. So, during her pregnancy, I took care of her as a husband, a mother, a nurse, a cook, and even an assistant. When she was in her seventh month, I took her to Atreyapuram, where some pre-delivery functions were performed. My in-laws came to our place with what is known as the Sudidalu and my parents went to their place later for a reciprocal function. By then I had dropped her off at her parents' place in Attili.

I went back to Bombay and kept in touch with her through letters, which was the main mode of communication then. I wasn't worried as she was in good health and was under her parent's care. The delivery went off smoothly and we were blessed with a baby boy on September 14, 1968. I was overjoyed and also relieved that mother and baby were fine. I conveyed the news to my friends and they were all happy for us. My wife's friends also congratulated me, asking me to convey the same to her. I distributed sweets among friends and colleagues.

I was very eager to go and see my wife and child. Soon after a baby is born, we hold a religious function called Balasala, in which the child's horoscope is drawn and a name is given. The date of the function was fixed for a month later and, accordingly, I went to Attili. My parents came from Atreyapuram with gifts for their grandson and daughter-in-law. They presented him with a gold locket, bracelets, a ring, and two silver molathadu and, of course, new clothes.

My son was named Suryanarayana after my father, as is our custom. The baby was active and fair and a little lean. All of us were very happy. My father-in-law's happiness knew no bounds.

He arranged a feast for all his relatives. I spent some time with my wife and child. We decided that they would come to Bombay after three months, so I returned home.

However, things were not meant to happen that way. I was deputed to undergo a training programme at RBI training college in Madras (now Chennai). After that, I was to undergo an important hands-on training programme at the ministry of finance, Government of India. The trainings delayed my trip to Attili to bring them to Bombay. Sadly, my wife had to listen to some uncomfortable comments from her relatives because of the delay. Some even cast doubts on my intent as I had married her without seeing her. Of course, all doubts were laid to rest when I went to Attili to bring them back. From there, we first went to my parents' place. All our relatives were happy to see our child. Then we visited Hyderabad where my sister lives. Finally, we came home.

Our friends demanded a party and we readily obliged. We started calling our child Suri and it became his nickname. He was growing up fast and learning things quickly. By the time he was 10 months old, he started walking, and a month later, he started talking. As soon as I'd come home from the office, he'd rush to me and I'd have to take him outside. I would indulge him as our residential complex had a good compound and an open area to walk. Some of my bachelor friends and colleagues would take him out to play as well.

Every weekend, we would have friends over. Sometimes, we would go to our friends' houses. They all loved Suri. There was no one to help my wife with her household responsibilities and she got very busy with the baby. So many a time, I'd help her out. I'd sing lullabies to put our son to sleep, but he'd want to play and not sleep. Things went on well and soon Suri turned a year old. We organised a birthday party, inviting all our friends and some of my colleagues. It was a nice gathering.

Every year, we would go to my parents' place and from there to my in-laws' place for a holiday. On the way back, we would stop in Hyderabad as there were no direct trains to Bombay from

Rajahmundry. We would stay at my elder sister's house there. My son was well-loved by all our relatives.

After more than two years, my wife was pregnant again. She was under the care of our family doctor, a woman, and was in good health. The doctor assured us that everything was fine. In the eighth month, I took her to Attili and left her in her parents' care. My parents too came there and attended her Seemantham, a pregnancy ritual. I returned to Bombay.

Soon after, on November 14th, 1970, she delivered our second baby boy. He too was healthy. On the 21st day, I went to Attili and my parents came and performed the Balasala ceremony. This time, the ceremonies were very elaborate as our baby was born under Lord Krishna's Janma Nakshatra. In keeping with our tradition, he was named Venkata Ranga Gopal Krishna Murthy after my father-in-law. We called him 'Gopi' for short and it became his nickname. My parents presented him with a gold locket, murgulu, a silver molathadu, and new clothes.

After the function was over, I returned to Bombay. Suri wanted to come with me, but I assured him that I would be back soon and take him, his tammudu (younger brother) and their mother. He developed a deep attachment to his brother. As promised, I went back to Attili and brought my family to Bombay in the third month. My second son had thick black hair and looked like a baby from ads. In fact, Glaxo approached us asking if they could use his photograph in some advertisement of Glaxo milk, but on the advice of some elders, we said no. Gopi was also very active but not a fast learner. He started walking when he was 10 months old but started to speak properly only when he was almost three. But after that, he picked up things very fast and was very friendly. Now, when I got back home from the office, I'd have to take both my sons out. I would hold them by the hand on either side and take them out to play.

My wife was keen to have a baby girl. But at that time, having two children was the norm and there was no guarantee that we would have a daughter. My wife strongly felt that we should have a girl child, only then would the house will be full of gaiety and joy, as girls represent the Goddess Mahalaxmi. Even as we were discussing the matter, the doctor gave us the news that she was expecting again. Our family doctor was on holiday and another female doctor was attending to my wife in her absence. So, there was some confusion about the delivery date. My wife felt it should be a particular date, but the doctor gave a date of two weeks later.

Meanwhile, my father had fixed the marriage of my younger brother, who was staying with me at that time. The wedding date was almost clashing with the delivery date as estimated by my wife. I, therefore, suggested to my father that he postpone the wedding by a few weeks. But that was not possible. We went to the wedding. My wife was already in an advanced stage of pregnancy and could not actively participate in the ceremonies, which she would've loved to do.

Soon after the wedding, we went to Rajahmundry to admit her to a maternity home. But the doctor there advised that we could go to her parents' place in Attili as there was enough time. On January 28th, 1972, a few hours after we reached Attili, she delivered a baby girl. My wife's happiness, despite the strain of the last few days, knew no bounds. God had answered her wishes.

Our daughter's Balasala ceremony was performed on the 21st day. She was named Lakshmidevi after my mother. My mother was very happy and gave her a gold necklace, some bangles, earrings, and new clothes. I brought them back home after the ceremony. We started calling her Lachi and that became her nickname.

She was extremely attached to me as she grew up. All my three children were very close to each other and had deep attachment to me, at times even more than their mother. My wife brought up my daughter in a traditional manner. She looked like a typical Andhra girl. She was growing up fast—she took her first few steps in her sixth month and was talking by the time she was one year old.

The young girls and elderly women in our colony would take her out and play with her. She was reluctant to go out and preferred to play in the house. Suri used to take Gopi to the complex grounds and play with other boys. He was very attached to his younger brother and even in his dreams, he would enquire where his brother was. My wife and I were very happy with our three children and their behaviour and affection towards us.

We moved to a bigger flat provided by the bank in the same locality. We had a happy and contented life. We were blessed with a large friends' circle and used to socialise with them on Sundays and other holidays, eating home-cooked meals and talking late into the evening. Our children were a constant source of joy. Every winter, we would go on picnics to places like Powai Lake, Vihar Lake, Titwala Ganesh temple in Thane, and Matheran. While other picnics were one-day affairs, we would go to Matheran for two days. These were fun times for the kids. My wife would celebrate our children's and her own birthdays by inviting friends over. We used to celebrate Ganesh Chaturthi and Deepavali at home. The children would participate with devotion and fervour. It was a time for feasting as my wife would make a variety of tasty dishes.

The time came to admit my first son, Surya, to school. We chose North Bombay School in Ghatkopar West. He used to go by the school bus. For the first few days, I went with him. But soon he started going on his own. Later, I got my second son, Gopal, admitted to the same school.

We'd dress up the boys in similar clothes. Since they were not too far apart in age, people would think they're twins. Apart from Atreyapuram, Attili, and Hyderabad, we went on a couple of pilgrimages as well.

But even as life went on smoothly, we had a couple of personal losses. My father-in-law suddenly died of a heart attack. He had been diagnosed with heart disease and was preparing to go to Vellore for a surgery. A couple of years later, in February 1976, my father too died of cardiac arrest when he was preparing to go to a village where we have some land. After their death, the frequency of our visits to our parents' homes decreased.

In June 1976, I was allotted an apartment by the bank in Prabhadevi and we shifted there. My first task was to get my sons admitted to new schools. We were told there were three schools in the area and decided on Raja Shivaji School (popularly known as King George School) in Dadar T.T. A colleague was also trying to admit his children to the same school. He and I met the managing trustee of the school to talk to him about their admission. At that time, schools used to take donations for admission of students. Since our children came from educated families, the managing trustee requested that we give a small donation of Rs. 300 each. We agreed and completed the admission formalities.

As Suri was already going to school, he was admitted immediately. In the case of Gopi, the headmaster wanted to interview him. He confidently answered all the questions in the interview and was granted admission. This time, I registered his name as Gopal Kasichainula, because the name given to him originally was too long. The boys would take the bus to school.

When it was time to send our daughter, Lakshmi, to school, we chose the Convent Girls High School adjoining Siddhivinayak temple, close to our house. The principal admitted her straight to K.G. She could walk to school as it was close by. Sometimes, when it would rain, I would drop her at school.

All our children were good at studies. Once they passed their SSC exams, both the boys were admitted to Kirti College to pursue their Intermediate in math, physics, and chemistry (MPC). Both scored first-division marks in the finals and we decided that they should pursue engineering. Surya got admission in Father C.R.College of Engineering (part of Father Agnel) in Bandra, Bombay. An acquaintance helped me secure admission for Gopal in Vivekananda Engineering College in Chembur, but he refused to join that college. I know he was a bit disappointed with his exam results. But soon, he got an offer from B.M.S. college of Engineering, Bangalore (now Bengaluru), and he agreed to study there. My wife, daughter, and I accompanied him to Bangalore when he went to join the college. My daughter did her B.Sc. (Microbiology) from Ruia College. Later, she did DMLT professional course.

A celebration of life

ৡ

My wife and children loved celebrations of all kinds. When the kids were young, we would celebrate their birthdays. They'd wear new clothes, my wife would cook delicious dishes, we'd decorate the hall for their birthday parties and invite their friends. There would also be songs and music to add to the festive atmosphere.

Then there were religious festivals like Ganesh Chaturthi and Deepavali, which we used to celebrate every year. Like my father, I would recite the puja mantras on Ganesh Chaturthi. Deepavali was a riot of colours, crackers, sweetmeats, and savouries. My wife would prepare snacks and sweets and distribute them among our friends. I would supervise the children as they burst firecrackers. I purchased a premier Padmini car for my family and personal use. Its original color was copper brown. I used to drive myself. It was very useful, particularly for social activities. Sometimes, I used to drop my daughter in college. I have taken the car to Ahmedabad and Calcutta also. I was using it extensively for my personal use. Of course, for official purposes I was using my office car. After my return back to Mumbai, there was not much use for it. After me, Surya was using the Padmini.

In April 1992, we completed 25 years of married life. That was another cause for celebration.

Our children had grown up by now and we had to plan their initiation into our religious order as per our customs. The first such event, in February 1993, was the Upanayanam (sacred thread ceremony of the Brahmins) of my elder son. Whenever we had to plan any such events, my wife and I would discuss things in detail—the ceremony to be conducted, the venue, the names and number of guests to be invited, gifts to be given, the caterers, etc. I would give her my budget for the event. After that, she would take care of the implementation. She was very good at such things. She knew the customs and rituals of our community very well.

At the time of Surya's Upanayanam, I was posted in Calcutta while my family was in Bombay. We decided to perform the function in Bombay. The venue was decided as Andhra Mahasabha. My sisters and their families came to Bombay to attend the event. My sisters and brothers-in-law wanted to visit Shirdi, the home of spiritual leader Sai Baba, and I arranged for their travel. At that time, my family stayed in Kandivali, where we had a flat.

Next was the Upanayanam of our second son. Many of our relatives complained that they could not attend Surya's thread ceremony because it was held in Bombay. So, we decided to celebrate Gopal's Upanayanam at my in-laws' house in Attili. In fact, according to custom, the ceremony is supposed to be held at the maternal uncle's house. Some of my son's friends also came to Attili with us and they were enamoured by the natural beauty of the region. The function went on very well and was appreciated by everyone.

The next major celebration was my eldest son's wedding. He had been working for a couple of years and wasn't planning further studies, so we thought of getting him married. We started receiving marriage proposals from Bombay as well as Andhra Pradesh. We thought a city girl would be a better choice for him and he agreed. We shortlisted three girls whose parents were well known to us. He chose one whose father happened to be a distant relation of mine. But we decided that the wedding would be held only after Lakshmi's wedding was finalised.

We started looking for prospective bridegrooms for our daughter. She was so attached to us that we thought any match outside India would not suit us. In those days, Indian students had started going to the US in large numbers either for higher education or for jobs in the IT sector there. We saw few good matches in Bombay, but they did not suit our requirements for various reasons. Finally, we pursued a match from Andhra Pradesh. My elder brother knew the boy's family very well and he highly recommended the boy. He was employed as a computer professional with a reputed company in Madras. My brother arranged for a meeting between Lakshmi and the boy and his parents at their house in Kakinada. The boy and girl liked each other, and we agreed to marry them.

There was a slight problem as I was in Calcutta and all the activity was happening in Bombay and Kakinada. My wife took a leading role in all the proceedings. My brother was the final word for us. The bridegroom's father suggested that the wedding should be held in Kakinada as they would not be able to come to either Calcutta or Bombay. We agreed to their proposal. I informed my son's would-be father-in-law that they too should organise the wedding in Kakinada. He readily agreed to do so as he too was originally from there.

My brother appointed a well-known priest near his house, who also happened to be related to my cousin sister, to conduct the weddings. Lakshmi's wedding was fixed for August 21st and Surya's for August 24th. The year was 1994. We booked Sri Venkateswara Kalyana Mandapam for two days for Lakshmi's wedding and the Railway Kalyana Mandapam for our son's wedding.

We wanted a grand wedding for our daughter. Every event—the marriage hall, decor, the music band, the catering, gifts for relatives, and post-marriage Ureginpu—was planned meticulously. My wife managed the event very well. We booked three hotels in Kakinada for our relatives and guests. We ourselves stayed at my brother's house. My son's wedding arrangements were also planned equally well.

A couple of months before the wedding, in June 1994, I was transferred from Calcutta to Bombay. Soon after, in 1995, Bombay was officially renamed as Mumbai. While I was in Calcutta, I had faced some health problems. I was finding it difficult to go for my morning walks and there was a heaviness in my chest. The doctor conducted many tests but could not diagnose the problem. After coming to Mumbai, I consulted the doctor from my bank. He referred me to a cardiologist. I was diagnosed as having blockages in two arteries and was asked to undergo a bypass surgery immediately. In those days, angioplasty was just emerging. We told him that I would get it done after my children's weddings.

We decided not to tell anyone about my medical condition. My wife took charge of things. Both the weddings were organised in a grand way as planned by us. We had more guests than we had anticipated. Some of my son's friends from Mumbai came for the wedding, adding some music, dancing, and cheer to the event. The families of our son- and daughter-in-law were very happy with the arrangements. We were really happy when an elderly lady complimented us for organising the weddings so well. She was the great-grandmother of my son-in-law, Prasad.

After the weddings were over, we went to Tirupati. The newlywed couples performed Venkateswara Kalyanam and we had a good darshan of Lord Venkateswara.

We hosted a reception for our friends in Mumbai who could not come for the weddings. The rains were on, so we booked an indoor venue in Worli. We had to restrict the number of invitees as the hall had a limited capacity. All the people we invited graced the occasion.

We wanted Gopal's wedding to be as grand as the other two weddings. Around the time we were planning the wedding, I was in Hyderabad at the Jawaharlal Nehru Institute of Development Banking (JNIDB). My cardiac problem resurfaced. A major blockage was discovered in an important artery. After tests, the doctors recommended an angioplasty, preferably at Apollo Hospital, Hyderabad; it had to be done immediately.

At that time, Gopal called me and said that he had selected a bride for himself and fixed the date and venue for his wedding as well. He wanted me to bless the union. The bride's maternal uncle also spoke to me on the telephone. I said they could go ahead with the wedding and asked my elder son and daughter-in-law to represent me. I also requested the hospital authorities to postpone my angioplasty by three weeks, so it would not clash with the wedding date. Accordingly, Gopal got married on January 6th, 1997, and my operation was held on January 27th. Soon after, the newlyweds came to our house and spent a few days with us. My wife hosted some post-wedding functions for them.

We were also blessed with a handful of happy and healthy grandchildren. Our first grandchild was a baby girl, born to Surya and his wife Suseela on February 19th, 1996. We celebrated her Balasala in Hyderabad in her third month. We invited my mother, uncle, aunt, sisters and their families, Suseela's parents, grandparents, uncles, and aunts, among others. We held a grand feast to mark the occasion and gave gifts to the guests. The girl was named 'Svikriti'. We presented gold ornaments and new clothes to our granddaughter.

On September 20th, 2000, Lakshmi was blessed with a baby girl in Detroit in the US. My wife had gone in advance for the delivery. I went to attend her Balasala, which was performed in the third month. Prasad's parents also joined in the function. The baby was named Pavani Annapurna. The priest who performed the function was from my in-laws' village but he settled in the US. It was a grand event with Gopal and his wife, my cousins Kumar and Dona, and Lakshmi and Prasad's friends in attendance. As usual, there was feasting, and we gifted gold jewellery and clothes to our granddaughter.

In 2003, Lakshmi had her second baby, a boy, and Gopal was blessed with his first baby, a girl. Lakshmi's baby was born on March 5th, 2003 and Gopal's daughter was born on June 24th, 2003. My wife went in advance to assist them with the deliveries. I too went to my daughter's place to help her look after the kids. Both the babies' Balasalas were performed at Sri Venkateswara Temple, Chicago. The functions were performed by the temple priests. The catering was done by some Telugu people settled there. The boy was named Vivek Ramakrishna and the girl Uma Mihira.

On November 10th, 2004, Surya and his wife had a second child, a son. We celebrated his Balasala at our Navi Mumbai house. All our friends and Surya's colleagues and in-laws attended the function. My brother-in-law, his wife, and son also came from Attili. We bought gold ornaments and a silver molathadu form Rajahmundry for the baby. He was named Sriharsh.

Our sixth grandchild was Gopal's second daughter, born on October 22th, 2006. The Balasala was held at his residence in Bettendorf, Iowa, in the U.S. Surya, who was working in Toronto, Canada, came for the event. We celebrated Sriharsh's birthday the day before the Balasala in Gopal's house. All our relatives were present. The Balasala was a grand one. All my son's friends and colleagues attended the function. Lakshmi and Prasad, along with his parents, came from Detroit to attend the function. The girl was named Vidya Mahima.

Six grandchildren meant as many birthdays and celebrations. We threw a big birthday party for Svikriti's first birthday in Hyderabad and invited all our close relatives. Svikriti's Aksharabhyasam was performed when we were in Cuffe Parade, Colaba.

Vivek's birthday and Sriharsh's Annaprasana were celebrated in my paternal village, Atreyapuram amid relatives and Vedic blessings.

On February 5th, 2012, my wife was completing 60 years of age, so we decided to perform her Sasthi Poorti in a fitting way. I consulted an Andhra priest and all the ceremonies to be performed and arrangements for the event were finalised. All our children, their spouses, and our grandchildren came to our Navi Mumbai residence for the ceremony. We also invited some of our old friends and some neighbours from our colony. The function went off very well. My wife gave gifts to our children and grandchildren. The guests were treated to a sumptuous lunch and gifts of clothing, sweets, and fruits on special occasion.

By now, Sriharsh was nine years old and we thought we should perform his Upanayanam ceremony. Accordingly, we consulted the local priest and fixed the Muhurtham on June 7th, 2014, at 9:21 AM. We got the invitation card printed in Hyderabad as per the design approved by my granddaughter. For the venue, we selected the community hall of our housing society. Arrangements for the stay of our guest and relatives were made nearby. My grandson followed all the rituals obediently and patiently. He was the darling of the guests, who numbered nearly 200. The function included Nadaswaram and recitations by vedic scholars.

My other grandson Vivek's Upanayanam was organised in Visakhapatnam, at his paternal grandparents' place.

My wife and I were married on April 26th, 1967, and we were to complete 50 years of marriage in 2017. We wanted to celebrate the occasion by organising a family get-together with our children and grandchildren and by performing the usual religious ceremonies. April wouldn't have suited our grandchildren as schools were on at that time in the U.S. Any date after June 10 would work for them. So, we fixed the anniversary celebrations for June 18th, 2017. The in-laws of our elder son and daughter were invited. Our second son's in-laws were settled in the US so they couldn't make it.

On the day of the event, we decorated the house. The purohit and his three assistants came at 8:30 AM and made all the arrangements for the ceremonies, namely Sri Ganesh Puja, Navagraha Puja, Ayushya Homam, and Venkateswara Deeparadhana. Gopal and Lakshmi came from the US along with their families a couple of days early. My granddaughter Svikriti, who was studying engineering in the U.S., also came for the occasion. Surya was in Dubai and he came from there. My elder daughter-in-law and grandson Sriharsh also joined us.

On June 18th, the ceremonies started at 9:30 AM and went up to 1:00 PM with just a half hour break. I wore a traditional silk dhoti and Angavastram. My wife wore a silk sari in a deep pink colour. She was also heavily decked in jewellery.

After the Ayushya Homam, there was the Poornahuti, where all participated enthusiastically. Venkateswara Deeparadhana was the concluding ceremony. Then there was Mangalarati. My daughter and granddaughters participated in it by singing and Sriharsh was the photographer. We gave our children, grandchildren, son-in-law, and daughters-in-law cash gifts. The in-laws of our children were presented with new clothes.

The last item on the agenda that day was the inauguration of this book by Shri N. N. Murti Garu. The book was still in manuscript form. It was titled; A Father's Legacy with the tagline Atreyapuram to Mumbai Megapolis—The exciting journey of a village boy. Murti Garu spoke well on the occasion.

In the evening, my grandchildren treated us to a musical show. Vivek compèred the programme. Svikriti and Sriharsh sang Telugu and Hindi songs, both classical and from films. Pavani rendered Hindustani classical songs in her beautiful voice. Vidya sang a classical Telugu song and Uma did an English recitation.

The main purpose of the celebration was to have a family get-together, and my children, their spouses, grandchildren, and others actively participated in the function and thoroughly enjoyed themselves, which made us very happy.

Gallery

My parents Shri. Kasichainula Suryanarayana and Lakshmidevamma

Myself and wife Sri Bhanumathi Devi

My family (photo taken on the eve of our silverjubilee marriage day)

Four brothers - Dr. Venkateshwarlu, Sundararam, Kameswara Rao and Dr. Krishna Murthy

My eldest son, Suryanarayan and family

My second son, Gopal and family

My daughter and family

Wife's Sastipurti Function

Wife's Sastipurti Function

Sriharsh's Upanayanam

Sriharsh's Upanayanam

Our Golden Jubilee Marriage celebration

Visit of Sri Sankara Vijayendra Saraswati Sankaracharya Swamji to our house

Ancestral home with my grandchildren

Shri Kasichainula Suryanarayana Shata Jayanti
Grandalayam function

*Shri Kasichainula Suryanarayana Shata Jayanti
Grandalayam Function*

Eye Camp at Atreyapuram

Our ancestral house at Atreyapuram

A spiritual journey across Incredible India

ಌ

Till the time I was in college, my travelling was limited to going with my mother to visit our relatives in Madiki, Kakinada, Tuni, and sometimes Achampet and Aryavatam. We would go on holidays or to attend functions at these places. But opportunities for real travel came only after I joined Karnataka University. Some of the travel was in the form of educational tours and others were personal holidays.

During an educational tour to Bangalore, we were shown the Hindustan Machine Tools (HMT) factory, Hindustan Aeronautics (HAL), Bangalore University, Vidhan Soudha, Lal Bagh, and the Bangalore Palace on the outskirts of the city. Two of my friends and I took permission and went to Mysore. While searching for accommodation there, we had a pleasant surprise. We went to a house where an officer of archaeology stayed alone. He invited us in, offered us some cold drinks, and asked us the purpose of our visit. When he got to know that we were students and did not have any source of income, he offered that we could stay in his house for free. Though he was Kannadiga, he spoke Telugu fluently. We visited the Mysore Palace, Chamundi hills, Chamundeshwari temple, Brindavan gardens, etc. Before venturing on the trips, I had bought a box camera for Rs 18 out of savings made from my monthly pocket money. We had a great trip and returned to Dharwar.

We went on another university trip to Goa after its liberation by the Indian Army in 1962. We took a bus there. Goa was really beautiful and we felt like we were in a foreign land. There were remnants of the Portuguese culture. While looking for accommodation, we met an IPS officer of the Andhra cadre who was on deputation to the Goa government. He suggested that we stay in his bungalow as he was alone. We went to beautiful beaches and bridges on the backwaters. The roads were good. The only problem we faced was food. Vegetarian food wasn't easily available; in fact, according to the locals, fish was vegetarian food. But we managed to get by—the leader of our group had brought plenty of chapatis and vegetable curries and shared that with us. We saw the Mangesh temple, St. Francis Church, where the body of the saint was preserved for nearly 400 years and his little finger was on display, and a few other temples.

My next two trips were personal ones. Three of my friends and I from the university went to see the ruins of Hampi, the Vijayanagara empire. We went by train and got off at Hospet. We first went to Anegundi, the original kingdom before Vijayanagara was established. It was a small place. The Raja was present there and spoke with us in Telugu. We went for darshan of the Virupaksha, Vijaya Vittala, and Krishna temples, etc. Except for the first one, all were in ruins. The towers of Virupaksha temple were very high. A large stone idol of Lord Ugra Narasimha guards the ruins. Another masterpiece is a stone chariot in front of the Vijaya Vittala temple. The Mahanavami Dibba, with a height of 25 feet and area of 80 square feet, is one of the most impressive structures in the area. Some of the other attractions were Lotus Mahal, Elephant Stable, the watchtower, and the Queen's bath. We also went to the Tungabhadra dam and gardens. The trip was really tiring but very interesting. We felt bad about the empire's collapse.

The second trip was a short one to Gokarna Kshetra. I went there by bus with two friends. In those days, there was no lodges or hotels to stay in. Only vedic scholars' houses were on offer for both lodging and boarding, but they were not accommodating of people of all castes. One of my friends was dark complexioned and his Upanayanam had not been performed. So, he was asked to eat his meals outside the house. But when he recited the Shiva Tandava Stotram, the host was convinced that he was a Brahmin and allowed him to eat inside. Gokarna Kshetra is the place where Shiva's atma-lingam had got stuck in the land while Ravana was taking it to Lanka. There was a beautiful temple there which houses the atma-linga; we were allowed to touch it. There was also a Ganesha idol in a standing pose. Veda Parayana was done every morning and evening. Apart from being a temple town, it was a beautiful scenic place with beautiful sea beaches.

After joining my job at the JNKVV in Sehore, Madhya Pradesh, I had many official visits to Jabalpur, Bhopal, and Indore, apart from Raipur, but there was no sightseeing involved.

In August 1965, I moved to Mumbai with my RBI job and in April 1967, I got married. Till January 1976, all our holidays were to Atreyapuram or to Attili, with the odd visit to Kakinada. However, we had seen a few places in and around Mumbai, including the Elephanta Caves, where we went by a steamer from the Gateway of India. In Mumbai, we visited the Mumbadevi, Mahalaxmi, Sri Venkateswara of Phanaswadi, Babulnath, Siddhivinayak and Titwala Vinayak temples. We mostly travelled in a group with our friends. We visited the beautiful hill station of Matheran once. The toy train trip from Neral to Matheran was very exciting and the route passed through stunning scenic beauty. Everyone in the group enjoyed the trip. While returning, we walked back. Everyone was stunned when my son Surya walked the long distance without any fatigue. We went on picnics to Powai lake, Vihar lake, Borivali National Park, and Kanheri caves. We used to go to watch Telugu movies in groups as well. Every year, we would go on the mandatory holiday to my parents' and in-laws' villages.

I also took my mother on two important religious pilgrimages in 1973 and 1974. As a devout Hindu, my mother wanted to go on Kasi and Rameswaram yatras. I asked my father to join us, but he was not too keen. My mother carried his towel as a symbol of his presence. We arrived in Varanasi by train and engaged a priest of Telugu origin to show us around. He arranged for our stay and boarding. There are certain rules one needs to observe during tirtha yatras—one is that one must sleep on the floor and two is that you can have lunch but need to skip dinner. I too observed both the rules along with my mother. The first thing we did was take a dip in the holy Ganges. My mother carried out some rituals to purify the body while bathing. I saw some boy's dead body floating in the water. The priest who was guiding us advised me not to look at such things and disturb my peace as it was common to throw dead bodies into the Ganges. After the bath, we walked through the city's narrow lanes towards the renowned Kashi Vishwanath Temple. We performed an abhishek there on the deity with Gangajal. Then we visited the Vishalakshmi Devi and the Annapurna Devi temples in the vicinity. Next to the present-day Vishwanath temple was the old temple that was destroyed by Mughal emperor Aurangzeb. He built the Gyanvapi mosque in its place. At around 7pm in the evening, there is an aarti held on the temple premises. It is a beautiful sight and can make one very emotional. We felt as if Lord Viswanath himself had descended from Kailash. We were told that the present-day temple was constructed by Rani Ahilyabai of Indore and that Maharaja Ranjit Singh had donated the gold that plates the spire. The next day, we visited a number of temples like Kalabhairava, Tilabhandar, etc. We also went to the famous Banaras Hindu University and saw the Vishwanath temple on the campus. We also went for a boat ride which enabled us to see all the ghats, including the Harishchandra ghat. On the third day again, we went for a dip in the Ganges. Then we visited Ramnagar, also known as Vyasakasi. We visited the Vyasa temple where Ganesha is depicted as writing the Mahabharata. From there, we went to the Kashi fort. We greeted the king, who reciprocated our greetings. Next, we went to former Prime Minister Sri Lal Bahadur Shastri's house. On the way there, we met an elderly gentleman wearing a coarse handloom dress. Our guide introduced us to him as Shastriji's uncle. On enquiry, he told that he got a pension of Rs. 28 per month and that was enough for him to get by. On the next few days, we went shopping. Kashi is famous for silk sarees. My mother bought a few saris, particularly for my wife and daughter. The shop-owner said that I need not pay immediately and could pay after the parcel was received at my place.

Our next pilgrimage was to Allahabad (Prayag) where the Ganges and the Yamuna merge and the Saraswati joins them underground or antarvahini. There too, both of us took a number of baths in the river and my mother performed religious ceremonies while sitting on the sand dunes.

Having completed our Tirtha Yatra, we went to Calcutta from where we were supposed to go on to Puri for a darshan of the Lord Jagannath. In Calcutta, we had a darshan of the goddess Kali at Kalighat where animals are sacrificed as an offering to the goddess. After darshan, we went to see the Victoria Memorial and its surrounding areas. We also passed through the Howrah bridge. We took an evening train to Puri and arrived there in the morning. We met a rickshawala who talked to us in Telugu. When I expressed my surprise, he said he was from Anakapalli in Andhra Pradesh. He added that as a large number of pilgrims were from Andhra, many people in the town speak Telugu. After settling down in our hotel, we went for a bath in the sea. The Puri beach is beautiful with real blue waters and tides. I took a bath with the assistance of a fisherman who put a tyre around me for safety. When the high tide came, my mother got worried as for a minute I was not visible. The fisherman also spoke Telugu. We had a good darshan of Lord Jagannath, his brother Balabhadra and sister Subhadra. We also partook the prasad at the temple.

The temple priests have been recording the names of visitors for hundreds of years; ours too were recorded.

We started our return journey from Cuttack station. We took the Howrah-Madras Mail. When we reached Tuni, a town in East Godavari district of Andhra Pradesh, my eldest brotherin-law came to the station, called me aside and instructed me that after reaching Rajahmundry, we should perform Gangapuja and other required follow-ups to the Tirtha Yatra and then go to Kakinda instead of Atreyapuram. He told me that my elder brother was not well and had a liver ailment. My mother was not aware of it. I did as instructed. My brother was very weak but recovered in due course. Then we left for Atreyapuram and did the Kashi Santharpana. When I went to my maternal uncle's house in Kakinada, my aunt was very angry with me for not taking my wife and children to the Tirtha Yatra. She said I was like my uncle as he had also not taken her on pilgrimage. She stuck to her view despite my telling her that it wouldn't have been a comfortable journey for my wife as our kids were very young. Finally, I assured her that I would take them on a pilgrimage when they were a bit older – many years later, I kept my word.

In 1974, we went on the Rameswaram pilgrimage, which included the Rameswaram temple dedicated to Lord Shiva and other temples in Tamil Nadu. We went to Madras Central from Rajahmundry and then from Egmore station to Rameswaram. At the time, a railway strike was on. The Railways authorities had taken extra precautions like a pilot rail engine accompanying trains and deployment of extra railway police. Rameswaram temple is situated on an island in the sea and we had to pass the Pamban bridge on the sea to get there, which was very exciting.

We bathed in the sea and my mother performed some rituals there. From there, we went to a nearby temple. Then we had a series of baths in the waters of wells on the temple premises. Interestingly, all the wells contained sweet water despite being in the middle of the sea. There were 21 wells, named after the warriors of Vanarasena and Lord Ram, his brother Laxman and his wife Sita. All the pilgrims were in wet clothes. We then entered the Ramalingeswara temple and did abhishek on the deity. There was another Lingam on the temple premises, which, according to tradition, was brought by Hanuman. My mother offered puja to Lord Ramalingeswara and to Parvathavarthini Devi. One interesting thing we saw there were stones that were floating on water. People believe that they're the same stone that were used for the construction of Rama Setu. Next we went to Navapashanam temple, where the navagrahas (nine planets) are situated in the sea. When we started the puja and pradakshina (circumambulations), there wasn't much water, but by the time we finished, we were in waist-deep water; undeterred my mother completed the rituals.

On our return journey, we travelled by bus. Before going on the trip, I had picked up some of the Tamil alphabets so I could at least read the nameplates on the buses. We went to Madurai to see the Meenakshi temple, located in a huge complex with two tall gopurams. There was also a deity of Lord Sundareswara. After darshan, we toured the entire temple complex. There were two lizards, one gold and other silver, which are said to wash off women's sins. Our next stop was the beautiful Nataraja temple in Chidambaram and we also visited Sri Venkateshwara temple.

From there, we went to Srirangam near Tiruchirappalli to see the Sri Ranganathaswamy temple, dedicated to Ranganatha, the reclining form of Lord Vishnu. The temple complex, which is on the banks of the river Kaveri, is as big as a fort. There are seven prakaras or enclosures. The temple prasadam was very interesting—coconuts offered by us were grated and given back to us as prasadam. After we arrived in Madras, we visited Pakshi theertham, where two eagles come to a hill temple and circle it. We were happy we could spot both the birds. My mother was very satisfied with the tirtha, and we started our return journey to Atreyapuram. On the way to Madras, an unpleasant incident occurred on the train. We were travelling in an unreserved compartment, which wasn't very crowded. Near Gudur, a group of people in army fatigues entered the compartment and started talking to the passengers. I was wearing an HMT watch which was newly introduced in the market. One of the men said he wanted to buy the same watch and would like to test how it fits him. Unsuspecting of anything, I gave it to him. He then said he would bring tea and snacks for my mother and disappeared. The other fellows then started snatching gold bangles and bracelets from babies. Then we realised they were thieves.

After reaching Atreyapuram, my mother performed the follow-up puja after the pilgrimage and the important Rameswaram yatra santarpana. My mother had a very sharp memory. While talking about the yatra to others, she would explain things in detail along with the names of all the places we had visited, right down to the names of all the 21 wells in Rameswaram. I also earned praise as a devoted son for having taken my mother on the yatras.

After my father's demise in February 1976, our visits to Atreyapuram reduced. That year, our visits were only for religious ceremonies;

visits to my in-laws house practically stopped as my father-in-law had also passed away.

Once I arranged a major trip using LFC Travels to take my wife and kids on a pilgrimage to Tirupati, Srikalahasti, Srisailam, Ahobilam and Mahanadi. I wrote in advance to the Tirumala Tirupati Devasthanams (TTD) and Srisailam devasthanams and booked. First, we went to Tirupati. In those days, there was only one ghat road. We took a bath in the pushkarani (water tank), had darshan of Varahaswamy, and then went inside the temple. Down the hill, we had darshan of Varadaraja Swamy. We also went to Alvelumangapuram, Srinivasa Kalyanapuram, and some pushkaranis in the hill complex.

Then we went by bus to Srikalahasti. We had darshan of Lord Shiva and Goddess JnanaPrasonamba. The temple complex was really big and well-made. We climbed up the hill of the hunter devotee of Lord Tinnadu. We rested for the rest of the day and we went on to Srisailam by bus.

Once in Srisailam, we freshened up in the Devasthanam accommodation, which was a big bungalow with a watchman. We went for darshan of Mallikarjuna Swamy and then for the kalyanam of Brahmarambika Devi.

While writing down our names as participants, I wrote my full name and place as Atreyapuram. The executive officer called me and enquired about my background. When he heard my father's name, he was very happy; he was the executive officer in Vadapalli Devasthanam when my father was the managing trustee and my father had treated him very well. As a mark of respect to my father, he arranged for my wife and me to be the chief patrons for the kalyanam. We were very touched by his gesture.

We spent some time seeing the gopuram and other gods and goddesses.

We also wanted to see Patalaganga, a sacred place in the backwaters of the Krishna river, and the hydroelectric power project there. We went to the bus stand and was talking to my wife about going to these places. The depot manager overheard our conversation and figured from my accent that we were from East Godavari. He was from Peddapuram town in the district. Since we had small kids with us, he wanted to help us. He instructed the driver and the conductor of the bus going that way to stop at a particular place very near the project, drop us there, and then pick us up again from the same spot on their return trip. Thanks to him we had a comfortable and nice trip to Patalganga and the hydropower project.

Our next destination was Mahanandi. We got accommodation in a bungalow there. It was evening by the time we arrived and the watchman cautioned us that the area was dangerous and we should be very careful of thieves. Once everyone was inside the bungalow, he would keep a cupboard to block fortify the back entrance. Worried, I couldn't sleep much. But, luckily nothing happened. In the morning, we went to Mahanandi temple. After bathing in the centuries-old water tank, we had darshan of Mahanandiswara.

From Srisailam, we went to Ahobilam Narasimha Swamy Temple, inside a forest area. We had darshan and spent some time at the temple.

My wife, and especially the children, enjoyed the holiday. They did not complain even though they were not that excited about visiting temples. My wife, a devote of Goddess Parvati, enjoyed the trip despite it being pretty tiring.

In this context, I would like to mention that we visited Tirumala six times. My first visit was during this pilgrimage; the second was when I was visiting a nearby place on official work. I had an interesting experience when I went into a trance during the Suprabhata Seva darshan at the temple. On my third visit, I took the steps from Alipiri, which took me four hours to cover. The fourth time, I went there again with my family after my son and daughter's weddings to perform Kalyanotsavam. The fifth visit was an official one—I had been appointed as a one-man committee to recommend ways to invest the TTD funds. The visit was very soul-satisfying as I got a chance to spend some time standing very near to the Lord. My younger brother was working near Tirupati at that time. He invited us to come and spend some time at his place. He even arranged for a special darshan of the Lord Tirupati, besides arranging our visits to Sri Kalahasti, Kanipakam, and the Sri Varasiddhi Vinayakar temple.

We went to Srisailam, Mahanandi, Ahobilam again when I was at the JNIDB, Hyderabad. During that trip, we went to the Mantralayam of Sri Raghavendra Swamy. It was somewhat crowded on that day, but we had satisfactory darshan. While returning from Kurnool to Hyderabad, we halted at Alampur to have darshan of Mata Jogulamba. The new temple was not ready at that time. We had a good darshan of the Lord and of Mata. I felt bad when the driver pointed out to the place where the original temple was—it had been destroyed and made into a kabristan (burial ground).

On one of the trips to Tirupati, we went to Chandragiri Fort, the last capital of the Hampi Vijayanagar Kingdom.

Our next long trip was to temples to the north Andhra Pradesh. We went to Hyderabad, and then to Bhadrachalam. We had darshan of Lord Rama and Sita at the Sita Ramachandraswamy temple. Then we went to the Godavari river and the village of Parnasala, 32 km from Bhadrachalam. From there, we took a bus to Vijayanagaram. We did darshan of Sri Suryanarayana Swamy in Arasavalli, and Sri Mukhalingam, Sri Kurman, and Sri Varaha Narasimha Swamy in Simhachalam. From there, we went to Chintapalli where my brother-in-law was a teacher. Even in summer, the weather was cool and pleasant there. We went to Vijayawada, did darshan of Sri Kanaka Durga and Panakala Narasimha Swamy. Both were enjoyable.

After I joined IDBI, the nature of our holidays changed due to two reasons. First, I no longer had the luxury of taking long leaves, and second, my children, who were growing up now, started protesting that I took them only to temples. So, we started visiting proper vacation spots. On one trip, we did a road trip to Nashik from where we went to Saputara, a nearby hill station. I took my car with a driver. In Nashik, we did darshan of Trimbakeshwar and visited the Godavari. I wanted to go up to the point on the mountain where the river originates. I started climbing up, and midway, I suddenly remembered that doctor had instructed me not to undertake steep climbs after my Tirupati climb. But I continued my upward journey and reached the spot. I felt fine. While returning from Saputara, our car broke down. It took quite some time to get it repaired. My son and the driver had to go Nashik and bring back a mechanic. Consequently, we cancelled our trip to Shirdi.

We went on a long vacation to Aurangabad, Daulatabad Fort, and Ajanta and Ellora caves. The children thoroughly enjoyed the trip. Daulatabad, which was originally called Devagiri, was famous as Muhammad Bin Tughluq, the sultan of Delhi in the 14th century, had transferred the capital from Delhi to Daulatabad. The fort, though small, looked impregnable. Aurangabad was replete with memories of Aurangzeb. We visited Bibi Ka Maqbara, a tomb dedicated to Aurangzeb's wife and a poor imitation of the Taj Mahal.

We also visited Grishneshwar temple in Aurangabad. The original temple was desecrated by Aurangzeb and the present one was constructed by Rani Ahilyabai. We offered our prayers there.

The Ajanta caves are Buddhist monuments cut out of rocks on a hill in Aurangabad district. Despite dating back to the first and second centuries B.C., they are still intact. Ellora, on the other hand is a Hindu temple carved out of a single rock and a UNESCO World Heritage Site.

We also went on some short getaways. One was to Nagarjuna Sagar dam. We went to Pratapgarh and Raigarh ports, which stand testimony to the great Maratha king Chhatrapati Shivaji Maharaj. The hill stations Matheran, Mahabaleshwar, and Lonavala were also on children's holiday list. The other temples we visited are Mahalaxmi Temple in Kolhapur and Panduranga Vittal in Pandharpur. Panduranga Vittal is the Maharashtrian state deity just the way Lord Venkateswara is to Andhra. Mahalaxmi temple is one of the 18 yoga peeths.

My transfer to Ahmedabad accorded me the opportunity to explore new places of interest, some on official trips and some on personal trips. There are three famous temples in Gujarat. First, we went to the Somnath temple in Saurashtra on the western coast of Gujarat. The temple, which had been desecrated multiple times by Muslim invaders like Mahmud Ghazni, had been beautifully reconstructed by Sardar Patel, the first deputy prime minister of India. The destroyed base of the old temple can be seen. The temple is on the sea coast and its surrounding area was peaceful. The second famous temple in Gujarat is that of Lord Krishna in Dwaraka. Dwarkadhish temple, as it is called, is at the edge of the sea. It was marvellous. I witnessed the Dhwaja Arohan or flag hoisting programme at the temple; it was a grand affair. From Dwarka, we went to Bet Dwarka, an island at the mouth of the Gulf of Kutch and visited some temples there as well. The third temple we saw in Gujarat was Ambaji. We also visited two other places of historical interest—Mahatma Gandhi's house in Porbandar and the Sabarmati Ashram in Ahmedabad.

I also had the chance to visit the Dilwara Jain Temples near Mount Abu, Rajasthan, with their stunning marble architecture. I also happened to go to Udaipur, the 'City of Lakes' in Rajasthan, for an official function and took the opportunity to see the fort, the lake, and other places of interest in the in the area.

While I was posted in Calcutta, we visited the charming hill station of Darjeeling. We felt as if we were floating in the clouds. The Queen of Hills, as the town is called, has a cool to cold climate, beautiful trees, snow-capped mountains peeking out of clouds, and stunning views of the Himalayas. We passed vast stretches of lush tea gardens on our drives there. My daughter dressed up as a local tea garden girl and posed for photographs. Among places of religious interest, we visited Dakshineswar, Sri Ramakrishna Mission, and Kalighat in Calcutta. We also have visited the beautiful AJC Bose Indian Botanic Garden with its giant banyan tree. Our visits to neighbouring Orissa (now Odisha) were also exciting. We visited the capital city Bhubaneswar and saw the Lingaraja temple there. According to history, there were over 1,000 temples in Bhubaneswar alone. We visited the Konark Sun temple, which, of course, is in ruins. The Lord Jagannath temple in Puri needs no mention; I had already been there with my mother. We spent some time there and at the Puri beach. We also made a trip to the Udayagiri and Khandagiri caves, Ashoka edicts in Dhauli hills, and some Buddhist temples. I visited Patna in neighbouring Bihar and Ranchi (now in Jharkhand) as well but didn't do much sightseeing there.

After I returned to Mumbai to work in IDBI head office, most of my travel, both official and personal, were to foreign countries. Apart from that, we went on two short trips with my son Surya and his family. One of the holidays was to Goa by car. We visited the beaches, temples, and other important landmarks, and then went on a night cruise on a lit-up ship on the Mandovi river. There was singing and dancing along with music. Most of the songs were Konkani. My granddaughter Svikriti had a lot of fun. Our other family trip was to Shirdi for a darshan of Sai Baba.

After retirement, I settled down in my paternal village, Atreyapuram. Since I went back there after many years, I wanted to visit a number of temples nearby. I started with my village—I visited the temples of Venugopala Swamy and Rukmini, Shiva and Rajarajeshwari, Mahalakshmi, and Vadapalli Venkateshwara. I also visited the temples of Jaganmohan Kesawaswamy in Ryali, Koppu Lingeswara Swamy in Palivela, Siddhivinayak in Ainavilli, and Mukteswara Swamy and Sri Laxmi Narasimha Swamy in Antarvedi. Another unique temple I visited was that of Saneeswara-Mandeswar at Mandapalli. All of us, including my son Surya, performed abhishekam there. Pancharama Kshetras are five ancient Hindu temples of Lord Shiva in Andhra. We visited them in two trips. We also had darshan of Sri Kukkuteswara Swamy and Pithambika at Pithapuram.

We also planned a visit to the Char Dhams, the four holy places which the Hindus believe will help them achieve Moksha and booked advance tickets through a travel agent at Delhi. However, just two days before the trip, the agent called to inform that the yatra had been suspended for a week due to heavy rain and landslides. He suggested that for the same amount, which I already paid to him, he would arrange for an alternate itinerary for us in and around Delhi. I agreed, and we proceeded to Delhi.

From Delhi, we went to Haridwar. There we spent time at Bhatruhari Ghat, where we bathed and saw the Ganga arati; it was an ethereal experience. We saw the huge idol of Lord Shiva and visited places of tourist interest.

In Rishikesh, we crossed the Laxman Jhula, the famed hanging bridge across the river Ganga and saw the temples on the opposite bank. There are many ashrams in Rishikesh and set amid the mountains, the place looked beautiful. From there, we went to Dehradun, now the capital of Uttarakhand. We did not stay there, but did a quick tour the city. Our next halt was Shimla, a hill station in Himachal Pradesh. Even though the roads are narrow and the terrain hilly, we had a very pleasant trip. We saw the secretariat, then rode horses to a peak from where we could see China and Tibet. We stayed in Shimla only for a day. Our next destination was Manali via Kufri. We stayed at a hotel that was managed by a Telugu man and he served us Andhra food. We visited some famous temples in and around Manali, including the famous Hidimba temple; on the same premises under a tree, there is a shrine dedicated to Ghatotkach, Hidimba's son. We went to Kulu where we went on horseback to the Rohtang pass. There was snowfall and initially, I was scared, but the horses were well-trained, and their owners assured us there was no cause for worry. My wife was more confident than me. It was a thrilling experience. We came back to Manali from where we went to Dharamsala, another hill station in the region, the next day. We visited the Tibetan monastery where the Dalai Lama stays. We had a tour of the monastery, including the house where he stayed. The spiritual leader was, however, on a foreign tour at that time. From there we went to Dalhousie, which was really a very beautiful place, And then to Katra near Jammu. We halted at a hotel overnight in Katra. The next day, we went to Vaishnodevi temple, a shakti peeth and a very popular temple in northern India on a hilltop. We went up on two horses, accompanied by the horse-owners, of course. Many were going up on the steep hill on horseback, even with children. After reaching the temple, we stood in a queue. The security was very tight. Pens, cameras, cell phones, or any electrical items were not allowed. We had to deposit these things and collect on our way out. There are three holy pindis (natural rock formations) representing Mata Saraswati, Mata Mahakali, and Mata Mahalaxmi. We did darshan and presented saree and other items to the goddesses. After we came out of the temple, we were served lunch by a voluntary group. We rested for a while and then we started our return journey. It was different and shorter route. It was cloudy throughout, but we were thrilled after the darshan and our spirits were high.

The very next day, we left for Amritsar in neighbouring Punjab. On the way, we saw the Jammu assembly building and the Jammu king's palace from the outside. In Amritsar, we visited the holy Golden Temple and spent some time on the pristine premises. We also visited Jallianwala Bagh, where the British had massacred hundreds of innocent civilians. We went to Atari on the India-Pakistan border checkpoint and witnessed the change of guard. Next, we went to Kurukshetra, which the Haryana government had developed as a tourist and spiritual spot. This is where the Mahabharata war took place. We visited all the temples and places there. We also saw the place where Lord Krishna had told the Bhagawad Gita to Arjuna. Afterwards, we went back to Delhi and then to Atreyapuram. It was an enjoyable trip.

I wanted to see some places of historical interest and show them to my wife as well. So, we planned a trip to Delhi and its surrounding areas. We arrived in Delhi and stayed in our guest house. We went and saw the Red Fort, which was the main residence of the emperors of the Mughal dynasty for nearly 200 years. We also saw the Jantar Mantar, the observatory, the secretariat buildings, and Raisa Hills. Then we went to the Qutub Minar, which was constructed with material collected from demolished Hindu and Jain temples. The next day, we proceeded to Agra. There we spent some time at the Agra Fort, Akbar Palace, the place where Shah Jahan was imprisoned by Aurangzeb, etc. Then

A Father's Legacy

we went to Fatehpur Sikri, an abandoned fort. The real attraction, of course, was the Taj Mahal. We spent some time touring the beautiful monument, the front gardens, and pools. It was a pleasant experience. My wife purchased saris made of Banana fibres made by jail inmates in Agra. From there, we went on to Mathura and Vrindavan. We saw the Krishna Janmasthan temple in Mathura where the Lalla, as Krishna is fondly known, was kept in a narrow place; we went to an adjoining Idgah as well. We also did a city tour of Mathura. Our next destination was Ayodhya, where there were tight security arrangements in place. We then went to Varanasi and to Sanchi Stupa and Sarnath. We then embarked on our return journey.

My wife had not seen much of Karnataka, so we planned a trip there as well. Surya arranged a taxi from Bangalore and hotel accommodation for us in some places. We went to Bangalore from Rajahmundry by train and stayed in our guest house. In Bangalore, we saw places of interest such as the Nandi hills, Lal Bagh, Vidhan Soudha, some temples, and the Art of Living headquarters. We then went to Mysore where we saw the Maharaja's palace. We also went to Chamundi hills, visited Mahishasura Vigraham and had darshan of Mahishasura Mardini. We also went to the beautifully lit Brindavan gardens. Then we proceeded to Belur and Halebeedu. The temple and its architecture were beautiful and captivating. On the way, we stopped at Shravanabelagola, which has a massive idol of Gommateshwara Bahubali. The weather was very pleasant. Our next destinations were Ooty and neighbouring Coonoor with their rolling tea gardens and cloudy skies. We spent two days there and then returned to Bangalore, from where we went to Hospet. After doing darshan of Virupaksha, we went on a trip to the Hampi ruins. By the end of the day, we were completely exhausted. The next day, we went to the Tungabhadra dam and fountains. That concluded our trip and we returned home.

While we were in Atreyapuram, our last pilgrimage was to the North and South Kasi Rameswaram circuit. This time, we first went to Ujjain where we did darshan of Mahakaleshwar. We got a chance to see the Vibhuti Abhiseka from very close quarters. We also did darshan of Mahakali and saw many important temples there. Then we went to Varanasi and spent nine days there as per the shastras. On the first day, we took a bath in the Ganges and offered puja at Kedar Ghat, as is the custom of Andhra pilgrims. We did darshan of Kedareshwar temple and went and prayed to Lord Viswanath, Goddess Vishalakshmi and Annapoorna Devi. There was tight police security in and around the temple. We devoted all the nine days to visiting various temples and places. Then we went to Gaya, where we bathed in the shallow waters of the Vaitarani river. We also performed the shraddha ceremony for all our ancestors in front of Gayasur. It was an elaborate process and I carried the list of our ancestors for ready reference. The belief is that if you perform the shraddha of your ancestors in Gaya, you need not perform the annual ceremonies. After finishing the ceremony and resting for a bit, we went to the Mangal Gauri temple, which was on top of a small hill. It is among the 18 yoga peethas. On our return trip to Varanasi, it was raining heavily. We just about managed to reach our hotel. The next day, we went to Prayag tirth and took a bath at the Triveni Sangam; we also did the shraddha ceremony here and donated alms for feeding the poor. At Prayag, we visited the Madhaveswari temple, which too is a yoga peetha. We also visited Bodh Gaya, where Lord Buddha received enlightenment.

Having completed our yatra, we went to Rameswaram. Here too, our yatra was smooth and successful; we bathed in the sea and in the 21 wells, besides doing darshan of Rameswaram. We took the chance to visit Abdul Kalam's ancestral house. Then we did Navagraha puja and returned to Madras and then to Atreyapuram. This was our last pilgrimage while in Atreyapuram.

We returned to our home in Navi Mumbai and settled down there. One day, a thought crossed my mind—we had not seen the famous temples and religious places of western Karnataka. So, we planned a visit there. We went to Udupi by train. There we had a darshan of Lord Krishna. We engaged a taxi for the two days and visited places of interest like Murudeshwar, Kollur

Mookambika, Sringeri Sharada peetham, Horanadu Annapurna devi, Dharmasthala Sri Manjunatha Swamy, the Kukke Subramanya temple, Mangalore Mangaladevi, and Sri Durga Parameshwari devi at Khatil. It was a deeply spiritual experience. In Sringeri, we did darshan of both the swamijis and sat through the Chandramouleshwara puja. The place was beautiful. During our travel through Horanadu, we passed coffee plantations, tea gardens, and coconut trees. We then returned to Mumbai from Mangalore.

Our many tours across India gave us the chance to visit the nine Dwadasa Jyotirlingas, 14 Astadasa yoga peethas, five Narasimha Swamy temples, Four Sri Krishna temples, and many other important Vaishnava and Shiva temples. We also visited the Pashupati temple in Kathmandu, Nepal. We visited more than 10 Dharmika kshetras, 10 historical monuments, and holidayed in 10 beautiful hill stations. We also visited 10 famous ancient forts and 10 beaches. The entire list of our travels includes more than 100 other temples.

Around the world

ॐ

I've had the opportunity to travel to quite a few foreign countries and visit many tourist spots and places of historical interest. A lot of these visits were official—IDBI, where I worked, deputed me to attend a number of seminars, conferences, and training programs, besides sending me on discussion and familiarisation visits to foreign lands. My travels for work took me to nine countries. My wife and I also got a chance to travel to three countries because our children were working and settled abroad. We saw two more countries in transit.

My first trip abroad was to Switzerland in 1990, when I was designated to attend a programme in Managing Finance and Control from June 17th-29th at the International Institute for Management Development (IMD) in Lausanne. There were many international participants, including two from India. I went to Geneva by air and took a local train to arrive in Lausanne. The area near the institution, situated on the bank of a lake stretching all the way from Geneva, was beautiful. The programme was very interactive and case-study oriented. The case studies all related to real, well-performing companies. I could participate in them actively because of my experience and familiarity with computers. The programme was insightful and introduced me to the way international executives handle things.

I was staying at a hotel near the IMD. For two days, the hotel manager observed that all I had for breakfast was some buttered toast and a glass of fruit juice. On the third day, he told me that they would charge only $8 instead of usual $18. For dinner, the hotel would arrange vegetarian dishes for me.

You can't visit Switzerland and not see its picturesque locales. So, I took some time off and went on a conducted bus tour to visit the world-famous Alps, Interlaken, Charlie Chaplin's house, and a chocolate manufacturing unit. I also took a train to Zurich and visited the huge shopping malls there.

As suggested by my boss, I visited the house of a senior colleague, who was working at United Nations Conference on Trade and Development (UNCTAD) in Geneva. I gifted them some puja material from Sri Sathya Sai Baba, which made his wife very happy. We had lunch together and talked about various issues. He also made some suggestions on the kind of souvenirs and gifts I could buy for my wife and children and for my bosses.

In 1996, I visited London for the first time, again on work. I was posted as Director of IDBI's training institute, the Jawaharlal Nehru Institute of Development Banking (JNIDB), in Hyderabad. We were designing and conducting training programmes for development banks in India and across Asia. Even though I was considered an excellent teacher and faculty member, I had no experience in designing and executing training modules. Therefore, the bank decided to send me for a fourweek programme on Trainer's Training at RIPA International, London, from February 23rd to March 22nd. Most of the participants were from Asia, many of them civil servants, while some others were from Africa. I participated actively in the class because of my past experience as a teacher. The course was very useful and helped me design new programmes and modify some existing ones at the JNIDB.

I had taken two days of leave to see London and had made prior arrangements for my wife was to join me there. Accordingly, in the last week of the programme, she flew to London. This was the first time she took an international flight alone. I received her at Heathrow International airport.

London is a great city for tourists. It is well-connected by an underground railway network and bus services. My training programme over, I was ready for sightseeing, excited about using a Pentax camera and a video camera that I'd bought in London. We saw everything there was to see in London—from the Thames River, Big Ben, Parliament House, Buckingham Palace, and Westminster Abbey to Tower Bridge, Tower of London, St. Paul's Cathedral, Trafalgar Square, British Museum, Natural History Museum, the World War II control rooms, Madame Tussauds and more. We found the Tower of London very interesting. It was an old historical fortress and showcased many articles belonging to the Royals. Of particular note were the collection of arms, armour, and crown jewels. It is also home to the Kohinoor Diamond and a host of gold ornaments and vessels.

It was lovely to sit in Trafalgar Square and watch hundreds of pigeons descend around us. There is a tower there known as the Nelson Column, named after of the Battle of Waterloo. We also spent some time at Westminster Abbey and St. Paul's Cathedral. We saw the change of guard at Buckingham Palace.

London is full of museums and we gained many historical insights while visiting them. When we were at British Museum, a group of foreign tourists came up to my wife and asked whether they could take a photo of her dressed in sari. She obliged them happily. We posed and took photos with the wax figures of various international personalities and Indian leaders like Mahatma Gandhi, Jawaharlal Nehru, and Narasimha Rao at Madame Tussauds. Another interesting place we visited was the underground World War II headquarters from where Winston Churchill led the war. We also stood at the Prime Meridian, which serves as the reference point for Greenwich Mean Time. It is the place the east meets the west and we stood astride the line with one foot each in the eastern and western hemispheres. We stayed at the YMCA Guest House in London.

The next day, we left for Frankfurt, Germany. Frankfurt airport has arrival and departure areas that are far apart and are connected by a monorail. We took a local train from the airport to the railway station and checked into a hotel nearby. We booked ourselves for a conducted bus tour that started from the station. Frankfurt was totally destroyed during World War II, but it's been marvellously

A Father's Legacy

reconstructed exactly the way it was before the war. We visited Frankfurt Cathedral, the only building that survived the war although its interiors were gutted. We also visited the house of popular German writer Goethe.

From Frankfurt, we took a train to Rome. I had booked two tickets from the Travel Corporation of India, which issued Eurail tickets. But I had to pay the sleeper charges, which was $100 per night. The train left in the evening and arrived in Rome early the next day. While on the train, the ticket checker took our passports and kept them. When I expressed concern over this, he assured me that this was the practice and we would get back our passports while disembarking at Rome station. I was relieved when we got our passports back!

After checking into a hotel and having breakfast, we went on a tour of Rome. Incidentally, Rome's correct pronunciation in Italian is 'Roma'. We visited many places of interest including ancient ruins, fountains, new buildings, and Vatican City.

We saw the Colosseum, a massive amphitheatre whose construction started in 72 AD and finished in 80 AD. An estimated 100,000 prisoners were brought back to Rome as slaves after the Jewish War and they were employed in the construction of the monument. Most of the Colosseum is now in ruins.

Next, we visited the Roman Forum in the centre of the city. A rectangular plaza surrounded by the ruins of important ancient government buildings, the Forum was the place where people converge for meetings, festivals, and ceremonies. We also visited the Fountain of Trevi, the largest Baroque fountain in Rome. People believe that whoever throws a coin into the fountain with his or her back to it will return to Rome. If you throw two coins, you're supposed to fall in love with an Italian, and if you throw three, you will marry the Italian! We also visited some local markets where my wife bought some beaded necklaces.

When in Rome, one can't miss out on Vatican City, the residence of the Pope for about six centuries (since 1377). Vatican City is an independent country—the smallest in the world— ruled by the Sovereign Pontiff. The Pope was on a tour at the time we were visiting.

From Rome, we went to Paris, France, again by train. It was an overnight journey. The next morning, we arrived at Paris Central Station and checked into a nearby hotel. We visited the famous Eiffel Tower, a huge wrought iron lattice tower on the Champ de Mars in Paris. We went right up to the top and had a panoramic view of the city. We also saw many historical monuments that are now government buildings. We couldn't miss the Louvre, of course. The stunning art gallery and museum houses thousands of artefacts dating from the prehistoric to the modern times spread over many rooms. It was difficult to cover all the rooms, so we saw only a few. Paris has sprawling, and attractively decorated shopping malls and we went window shopping.

We really enjoyed our European sojourn, even though it was hectic. We flew back to Mumbai from Charles de Gaulle Airport in Paris.

In 1999, I was assigned to attend a conference on Managing the Global Economy in the light of the Asian Crises, again in London. The event was held from March 16-18 and organised by Wilton Park, an international forum for strategic discussion. There were interesting discussions on the then Asian crises. I made a presentation on how India could protect itself from the crises with prudent policies, which could be useful for other countries as well. I reached the venue, which was an old castle near London, from Gatwick Airport, the second airport in London. There was another participant from a Rating Agency. As I had already seen London, I did not plan any sightseeing. However, I met some officials of the Bank of England and held discussions with them on their policy framework and also visited the Bank's currency and coin museum. I also made use of the visit to hold talks with officials of Barclays Capital and HSBC Capital Markets.

From London, I went to Frankfurt, as per my itinerary. Frankfurt is an economic hub and has over 240 banks. I held an important meeting there with the President of the European Central Bank

(ECB), which is headquartered in Frankfurt. First, he briefed me about the formation of the European Union (EU) and the ECB and their activities, their common currency, the Euro, commerce and industry, and how to balance the inflation rate of various member countries. Then he answered some questions I had for him. In between, I briefed him about IDBI's activities and the purpose of my visit. He also asked me questions about RBI when he got to know that I had worked there earlier. The meeting went on longer than expected and was very insightful.

I also met officials from the Economic Research Department of Deutsche Bank and had a long discussion with them about their activities. I briefed them on our research activities. They appreciated our work. I met officials of Commerzbank as well and we talked about their operations and future plans.

While in Frankfurt, I was cautioned about a sect known as 'Redheads' who used to style their hair like ancient Roman warriors. I was told they were against Asians and could get violent towards them. I was advised to avoid them if ran into any. On my way back to my hotel, I did see two of them, but I evaded them by going into a basement shopping complex near the station.

In October 1999, the Mexican Development Bank was celebrating 65 years of operations. IDBI chairman was invited to participate in the celebrations and present a paper on the small and medium enterprises (SME) sector in India. He recommended my name in his lieu. The organisers wanted a PowerPoint presentation. I did my research, mainly from Small Industries Development Bank of India (SIDBI) publications and discussions within the bank, and prepared a presentation, which was then emailed to the Mexican Development Bank.

I was also sent to Mexico City to attend the event. The celebrations were organised on a grand scale. The reception was very good, and my dietary needs were taken special care of. Specialists from different countries and organisations, including the World Bank, participated in the event. My presentation was well-received, and the audience asked me a few questions, which I answered confidently. The organisers and the World Bank executives came to me and congratulated me for a really informative presentation.

Mexico was home to the ancient Mayan civilisation, which developed highly sophisticated art, especially stone sculptures. I went on a tour of the city and its outskirts and saw some cathedrals and colonial cities like Merida and Campeche. Mexico City is a nice place and very green. I had been advised to be careful as there were antisocial gangs operating in certain areas, but luckily, I didn't face any problems.

In 2000, the bank sent me to Cartagena, Columbia to present a paper at the International Seminar on Development Finance (May 18th-19th). Cartagena (pronounced Kartahina), lies on the sea coast. Columbia was a Spanish colony, and after independence, Spanish continued to be the spoken language here. The hotel where I stayed was on the seafront. The conference went well and my paper on the 'Role of development financial institutions' was well-received.

In the evening, the organisers took us on a city tour by a bus which looked like the old Bobbarlanka-Amalapuram buses back in Andhra Pradesh. Each one of us was given a bowl made of leaves to be worn as a garland. The purpose was that they would pour wine in it. Two of us were excused from the ritual at our request. There was singing on the bus and dancing after we got down. I sang some Telugu songs and recited some poems. The bus went through the main streets of the city, stopping at important historical monuments. Finally, by midnight, it reached the starting point near my hotel. Columbia is not a safe country and we were advised not to go out alone, but I had a wonderful time there.

In the same year, the World Economic Forum organised the Ninth Asia-Pacific Economic Summit 2000 in Melbourne, Australia, from September 11th-13th. I was deputed to attend the summit. The theme of the summit was 'Asia-Pacific in the 21st century: Leveraging the new drivers of growth'.

The summit brought together the top business and political leaders, industry experts, and opinion-makers from the region to enable them to brainstorm and assess the new landscape. There were seven-eight participants from India, including a minister. Sessions were being held simultaneously, so I selected some interesting sessions that I wanted to attend. The sessions were structured in such a way that there was a brief presentation by selected representatives followed by a question-and-answer (Q&A) round; I asked some pertinent questions during the Q&A.

There were massive demonstrations going on in Melbourne during the course of the summit. Anti-globalisation groups from the world over had converged in the city and they even tried to block the delegates from entering the summit.

The event was held at a big seven-star hotel while the delegates were put up in different hotels. I was staying at a nearby hotel along with many others. On Day 1 of the summit, we could not reach the venue because of the protests. So, the organisers made alternate arrangements. The hotel where the summit was being held was on a riverside. We were taken by bus to a point along the river and then taken by launches to the venue! The agitators were shouting slogans from the other side of the river. There was tight security cover to ensure no untoward incidents take place. The conference went smoothly. In the evening, we were taken back to our hotels by the normal route as by that time most of the agitators had left.

The agitation continued the next day as well, but the intensity had come down. I was walking down towards the venue when three agitators approached me and wanted to interview me. They identified me as a delegate by the conference bag on my shoulder. I managed to dodge them by saying that I was only a participant and that they should approach the organisers.

The schedule of the summit was tight, and I did not have much time for sightseeing. However, I squeezed some time out and went on a quick tour of Melbourne. The city is wellplanned and looked like a bigger version of Kakinada with all straight roads from east to west and north to south. It was a great experience to meet so many delegates from various countries and interact with them.

On the way back, I halted in Singapore for some meetings. The Development Bank of Singapore (DBS) was transforming itself into a universal bank operating in the Asian region. My bank had suggested that I talk to senior DBS officials about their plans and explore the possibility of a tie-up with us. Accordingly, I held detailed discussions with various departmental heads at DBS. They also showed me a PowerPoint presentation on their plans. The discussions were fruitful and we decided to pursue the matter further at a later stage. They were interested in some sort of tie-up, but it was too early at that stage.

I had planned to spend two days in Singapore. On the day of my arrival, there was a minor fire at the hotel and all residents were evacuated. We spent some two hours outside until we were allowed back into our respective rooms.

On the second day, I went on a city tour and saw the Parliament House, the Supreme Court, and the City Hall. I also visited Chinatown, which has traditional Chinese temples and shops. I went to Little India as well, with its famous Kamala Nivas restaurant, jewellery shops, and flowers gardens with jasmine blooms. It looked like a mini South India. I ate some snacks there and noticed that many people were eating with their hands, south Indian style. There are many other tourist attractions like the night safari, Jurong Bird Park, the zoological garden, museums, etc, but I neither had the time nor the interest to see them. I enjoyed exploring the large and beautifully maintained Changi airport in Singapore while flying back to Mumbai.

In 2001, I got a chance to visit Tokyo as I was designated to attend the 73rd Industrial Finance Seminar organised by the Industrial Bank of Japan from March 5-10. There were participants from Russia and Saudi Arabia, some Southeast Asian countries, Europe, and Australia. The focus of the seminar was the status of the world industrial development at that time and likely directions in the future.

I got down at Narita International Airport (originally New Tokyo International Airport) and stayed at the same hotel where the conference was being held. After the conference, a sightseeing trip was organised. They took us to Mount Fuji, an active volcano about two hours from Tokyo. The highest peak in the country at 3,776 metres, Mount Fuji has been a pilgrimage site for centuries and holds a special place in the hearts of the Japanese people. It's changing faces vary with the view, the time of day, the season, and weather, making for a stunning sight.

We also went to Kamakura, which was once the seat of the feudal government. There is a famous Buddha temple there dating back to 1252 AD, which houses an Amida Buddha statue. In 1498, a tidal wave swept away the great temple, leaving only the foundation stones. But the statue survived the natural calamity. It is 11.3-metre-high and weighs 121 tonnes. We had lunch at Kamakura—pure vegetarian temple food. We sat on the floor and ate our meal, similar to the traditional Maharashtrian way of eating. Later, we went to the downtown area. Tokyo is a very densely populated city with different modes of transport— underground, over-ground, and above the ground. I enjoyed the trip both for the seminar and the sightseeing.

Around this time, the Nepal Development Bank (NDB) was looking for financial and technical collaboration with IDBI. Their officials visited our headquarters and held discussions with our chairman and other senior officials. They invited us to Kathmandu for further talks with their senior officials. Our chairman deputed me and the bank's legal advisor to visit Kathmandu for an assessment. We arrived there in February 2002 and held meetings with the NDB officials. Their operations were mainly in the area of small enterprises, with some work in the medium sector, whereas ours was mostly in the medium and large sectors. So, we told them that the SIDBI would be a more appropriate organisation to help them.

We visited the famous Pashupatinath Temple in Kathmandu and had a satisfying darshan. The authorities presented us with rudraksha malas made of beads in three different sizes. We also toured the Himalayan mountainside and saw the Annapurna peak.

That was my last foreign visit before retirement. All the other trips we made to foreign countries were in a personal capacity, mostly to visit our children, who were working and living abroad in different countries at different points of time.

My younger son, Gopal, had gone to the U.S. for an M.S. programme in engineering and had successfully completed it from University of Iowa and joined a job there. He wanted both of us to visit the U.S. and in 1998, he sent us the flight tickets. To break the long journey, we first went to Detroit from Mumbai. From there we went to Ypsilanti, Michigan, where our daughter and son-in-law were staying. We stayed there for over two months, from June 27 to September 30. Gopal and his wife, Radhika, joined us for a few days. They took us on a tour of New York City and Washington DC. In NYC, we saw the Statue of Liberty. We took the steamer on the Hudson River and went to the historic Ellis Island and Liberty Island, where the statue is installed. The copper statue was a gift to the U.S. from the people of France and is an icon of freedom and of the U.S. We roamed the area and took photos and videos.

Then we went to see NYC. We were thrilled to travel by the vehicular tunnel under the river. NYC's skyline is outlined with tall buildings. We saw Manhattan and Empire State Building, which was once the tallest building in the world. We went to the top deck, which offers a stunning view of the city. We walked in the neighbourhood of the WTC twin towers, which were still standing then. We were really sad when they were destroyed by terrorists on September 11, 2001. We also went on a tour of NYC aboard an open double-deck bus. As we were reaching Wall Street, the bus had a minor accident and could not proceed further. So, we walked to where my son's car was parked. We also went to New Jersey.

We had a memorable visit to the U.N. Headquarters in New York. We explored the premises, spent some time in the General Assembly hall and the Security Council meeting hall and took some photos.

A Father's Legacy

Our next destination was Washington DC. Our first stop was the White House. Then we went to Capitol Hill and saw the U.S. Capitol Building, the seat of the U.S. Government. We also visited Lincoln Memorial, a national monument built to honour the 16th U.S. President, Abraham Lincoln. Two of Lincoln's well-known speeches are inscribed here and a large, seated statue of the president is installed. We also visited the Washington Memorial, with its tall pillar and some government department buildings like the Treasury Department, the Federal Reserve, and the Old Secretariat building. We also did a quick tour of the American History and Science Museum.

My son-in-law, Prasad, took us on a tour of Cleveland, Ohio, and the Niagara Falls. In Cleveland, we saw the famous SeaWorld theme park, where dolphins are trained to do acrobatics in a large pool; there are also shows by sea lions and other trained animals and birds. From there we went to Niagara Falls. The road journey to the waterfalls was beautiful. In the plains, the road runs almost parallel to the Niagara River. The river, which gets its water from the melting of snow in the hills, freezes over in winter. Finally, we reached the edge of the river, which falls into a deep valley.

The crashing waters of the falls made for an awe-inspiring sight, and the locale was beautiful. Visitors could climb right up to the edge to the Cave of Winds and see the falls from close quarters. We were provided yellow raincoats and special footwear. Our guide led us on an adventure over a series of redwood decks that brought us up close to the Bridal Veil Falls, only 25 feet from the cascading waters. After coming down, we went on an exciting boat ride called the Maid of the Mist, which took us right in front of the falls and to the base of the Canadian Horseshoe Falls. They gave us light blue-coloured raincoats, which we kept as souvenirs. We also saw the Canadian side of the falls while travelling in the boat.

In mid-July, Gopal took us to his place in Bettendorf, Iowa. His house was situated against the backdrop of a rolling landscape, lush with trees. We did a lot of sightseeing from here as well.

He took us to the Balaji temple in Chicago, a beautiful temple maintained by people of Andhra origin. We also saw Chicago, one of the biggest cities in the U.S., dotted with tall towers. We visited the 110-storey Sears Tower, which was once the tallest building in the U.S. Sears Tower stands second tallest in the country now. It's 1,454 feet tall, and with the twin antennas atop the building, its total height is 1,707 feet. We went up to the sky deck, from where we had a panoramic view of Chicago. We also went to some local markets.

I wanted to see the building where the Parliament of the World's Religions was held and Swami Vivekananda delivered his famous speech. But we could not get precise information about the location. We also went to Chicago's Little India, where sections of a road called Devon Avenue have been given secondary names like Gandhi Marg and Mohammed Ali Jinnah Way. There were many Indian shops and restaurants there. We then went to a place known as Navy Pier, a 3,300-feet pier on the shoreline at Lake Michigan. We travelled by boat along a narrow river lined with buildings on both sides. Aboard the boat, I opened my wallet to take out something. My son cautioned me not to do so as mugging was common in such places.

Next, he took us to my cousin Dr. Kumar's house in Dayton, Ohio. My daughter and son-in-law also joined us. Kumar was a senior scientist in NASA. His wife, Dona, was very hospitable. She cooked special vegetarian meals during our stay. Their two daughters, Effy and Suri, were very close to my son. While we were staying in Bettendorf, Gopal also took us to the University of Iowa where he did his M.S. That was the last place we visited on that trip before returning to Mumbai.

On this U.S. trip, we had taken a KLM-Northwest flight,. We had a seven-eight hour wait at Amsterdam for our connecting flight to the U.S. So, we took a visa and went on a guided tour of the city from the airport. Amsterdam is almost at the sea level, and a number of canals crisscross the entire city. We saw a windmill which was still in operation. Next, we were shown a cheese-making unit where the entire process was demonstrated. They also took us to a diamond-cutting and polishing unit where visitors could purchase diamonds. Once our tour was done, we took our connecting flight to went to Detroit.

In the year 2000, Surya was posted in Abu Dhabi by his company. He suggested that his mother and I should come and spend some time with them. We decided to go around the time of our granddaughter Svikriti's fourth birthday. My wife went on February 16th and I joined her on February 26th.

Surya took us on a tour of UAE or the United Arab Emirates. It comprises seven emirates. Abu Dhabi is the capital and Dubai is the second largest emirate and a leading centre for business and tourism in the Middle East. Sharjah, Ajman, Umm Al Quwain, Ras Al Khaimah, and Fujairah are the other emirates. Dubai is the main centre and is a shopper's paradise; Dubai Shopping Festival is a major attraction. They have a huge market for gold and diamond jewellery. We went to buy a pair of gold earrings for Svikriti's birthday. Her grandmother, mother, and aunt had all come along to help her select a pair, but the little one chose a pair she liked and wouldn't listen to anyone's suggestions. We went for an evening tour of Dubai and watched a laser show. My son also took us to a few other places, among them a popular oasis. The way was dotted by date palm trees—dates are very popular in UAE.

We celebrated Svikriti's birthday with her friends, Surya's friends, and other people in attendance. The little girl was already picking up Arabic numbers and a few words. She wore a new dress and her new gold earrings and enjoyed the birthday party.

The roads of Abu Dhabi were neat and clean and dotted with fountains. They were well-lit at night. I used to go for morning walks, and every day, I would choose a different road and walk to the end of the road and back. In the process, I must have covered the entire city area.

Interestingly, the colour of the sand is different in each of the seven emirates, and there are souvenirs—sealed glass containers—showcasing the sand. I bought one. I was also surprised to learn that the average lifespan of buildings there is 15-30 years, due to the harsh climate and humidity. They have to be demolished and reconstructed regularly. We enjoyed our stay in Abu Dhabi and returned to India in mid-March.

Around the same time, our daughter Lakshmi was expecting a baby and my son-in-law Prasad requested that her mother go to the U.S. and stay with her for a few months. Accordingly, my wife went to Detroit in June 2000. Lakshmi delivered a healthy baby girl on September 20. Her Balasala was scheduled for the third month and I reached the U.S. on November 18, 2000. My wife's acquaintance from Attili, Sri Shastri, was the priest for the ceremony and he conducted it in a systematic and elaborate manner. I also joined him in reciting the Namakam, Chamakam, and other stotras.

The baby girl was named Pavani Annapurna. Prasad's parents also attended the function, as did Gopal and Radhika. My cousin Kumar and his wife Dona, and Lakshmi and Prasad's friends were also there. We returned to India soon after the function while Prasad's parents stayed back to look after the mother and newborn. We didn't get much time for sightseeing on this trip; we just saw the Henry Ford Museum and explored the neighbourhood.

In 2003, Lakshmi was expecting her second child, so my wife left for the U.S. in end-January to look after her. She delivered a baby boy on March 5, 2003 and I joined them a little later, in end-March.

My daughter-in-law, Radhika, was also expecting. We went to their house in Toledo, Ohio, in end-May 2003. There was some tense moments at this happy time as Gopal was facing a health problem and had to undergo some treatment. My wife stayed back for my daughter-in-law's delivery. Radhika had a baby girl on June 24th, 2003.

Meanwhile, I returned back to Detroit to look after Lakshmi's children so she could return to work. I babysat our newborn grandson. Pavani was very playful and she thought her brother was a toy to play with. I had to keep a watch on her as well.

We decided to hold the Balasalas of both the newborns at Sri Venkateswara temple, Chicago. Apart from colleagues and friends of both our children and their spouses, the function was attended by Prasad's parents, my cousin Kumar, my nephew Nagesh, Murali and his wife. Our grandson was named Vivek Ramakrishna and granddaughter was named Uma Mihiri. After spending some more time with our children and grandchildren, we returned to India on 10th July, 2003.

During this last visit to the U.S., I had booked tickets on Aeroflot Airline to Moscow and then to Detroit. Since we had a long layover, we took sightseeing visas from a company that conducted city tours from the airport. We went to St. Peter's Square and explored the surrounding areas, which was the headquarters of erstwhile U.S.S.R. There were many buildings with domes and structures that looked like churches. The guide told us that some of them were really churches before the Russian Revolution.

He took us to a new church. He said it had originally been a church, but Stalin had demolished it and converted it into a swimming pool! Later, again, a church was built at the spot. It started snowing while we were there. By 3:00 PM, everything was dark. Our guided tour continued, though, as all places were well-lighted. We had a brief ride on a local train. Practically no one spoke English there. Our city tour over, we were dropped back at the airport.

In 2006, Surya was posted in Toronto, Canada, and we planned to visit him. We went to Detroit in August and applied for a Canadian visa from there. Surya and Gopal came over with their families to Lakshmi's house in Detroit—they had moved there from Ypsilanti. We celebrated Ganesh Chaturthi there. Then we went to Toronto.

The city was beautiful. We visited the Ontario lake and the CN Tower, a 1,815 feet-high communications and observation tower in the downtown. The top floor had a glass floor on which we stood and looked down at the city below—it was exhilarating and scary at the same time. We explored the downtown area, where all the commercial establishments were located. I would use the railway pass to travel by local trains to different places. We saw some other places of interest as well, like the Ontario Science Centre, Casa Loma, Royal Ontario Museum, African Lion Safari park, etc. We also went and saw the Niagara Falls from the Canadian side.

Svikriti was studying in a school nearby. She had a friend named Imogen. I used to accompany them to school. Svikriti did well in her studies and even won a prize for the best performance among new foreign students. Our grandson, Sriharsh, was growing up quickly and was very active. He would accompany me on my morning walks and play with the sparrows in the area.

It was time for us to go back to Detroit, to Lakshmi's house. We went there by road and stopped by the Lord Venkateshwara Temple and also saw the Carnage Science Centre, both in Pittsburgh, U.S.

We arrived in Detroit from Toronto in time for Pavani's birthday. Prasad and Lakshmi had engaged a professional event manager and Pavani's birthday was celebrated on September 24. There many friends of Lakshmi, Prasad, and Pavani at the party and all seemed to be having fun. Gopal also came down on the occasion. It was time for Surya to go back to Toronto, but by now Sriharsh had become very attached to me. When he saw that I hadn't got into the car, he kept asking me to come and sit in the front seat. He was disappointed when I didn't, which left me sad as well.

Prasad took us for some sightseeing. We went to Vivekananda Monastery, where we saw the prayer hall and other places. He also showed us the first centre of ISKCON, which was a big house donated by an English devotee. We also went to the Mystery Hill, where we saw many astonishing things that seemed to defy the laws of nature. The law of gravity does not work here. Water flowed upwards and we had a difficult time maintaining our balance. Many theories have been offered such as earthquake, magnetic mineral deposits, fallen meteorites, deflection of gravitational force, and others to explain this strange phenomenon.

From Detroit, we went to Gopal's home in Bettendorf. Radhika was expecting her second child. We were blessed with another granddaughter on October 22nd, 2006. The Balasala was fixed for 19th November, 2006. Lakshmi, Prasad, and their children came from Detroit. Surya's family came from Toronto. On 18th November, 2006, we celebrated Sriharsh's birthday in Gopal's house. The Balasala was scheduled for the next day. A priest from Sri Venkateswara temple, Chicago, performed it. Before that, he performed Yagnopaveetha Dharanna for both Surya and Gopal. The function was attended by colleagues of Gopal and Radhika. Kumar too came with his daughter. There was a sumptuous lunch prepared by a local Telugu family. The child was named Vidya Mahima. After nearly four months in Canada and the U.S., we returned to India in November 2006.

It was almost four years since we'd last visited the U.S. In the intervening time, the children had come to Atreyapuram twice and spent time with us. We had a great time with our grandchildren. Gopal had been asking us to plan a trip to the U.S. Finally, we decided to go. We left Mumbai on May 7th, 2010. By now, Gopal was staying at a place called Cedar Falls, which was in somewhat interior Iowa. So, we had to arrive in Minneapolis and take a connecting flight to Cedar City. But we missed the flight and had to spend some eight hours at the airport before taking the next flight. Gopal received us and took to his house in Cedar Falls. It was a small place but quite picturesque with the Cedar river crisscrossing the area. He showed us his factory unit in Waterloo. Srinivas, Radhika's brother arranged tickets for the lecture by His Holiness the Dalai Lama. He was visiting the local university. We had missed seeing him in Dharamsala many years ago, now we had a chance to see him and hear him speak. We also went to Srinivas's house and spent a day there. His parents were also staying with him. Pam, his wife, was very warm and hospitable.

Gopal had arranged a series of visits for us to California, Hollywood, San Francisco, and Los Angeles. My cousin Dr. Krishna Mohan (Babu) and his wife Annapurna invited all of us to come and stay with them. We went to San Francisco via Denver. We hired a car and went to my cousin's house, a spacious bungalow with a beautiful garden. Krishna ran a dialysis hospital along with some of his friends. His wife was my cousin from my father's side; she was very friendly. They had three daughters, all of whom were studying at that time.

Our first visit was to Hollywood. We went to the top of the hill with the famous 'Hollywood' sign, which can be seen from a distance. Then we went to Universal Studios, where we watched a 3D film for the first time. Gopal's daughters loved the trip; they even got their portraits made by a local artist. One of my close friends who lived in California with his son had invited us for lunch. We spent some time at his place and I invited him with his family to our cousin Krishna's house, of course with their consent. He came with us and we had a great time.

Gopal also took us to the famous Golden Gate Bridge; we crossed it and went to the other side. We spent some time near the seashore where a large number of walruses were resting. We did a long city tour of Los Angeles and had lunch in an Indian restaurant. We returned to Cedar falls, tired but happy.

Meanwhile, Prasad and Lakshmi's Detroit house was being repaired and they were staying in transit accommodation. We, therefore, did not plan a visit to their place. Instead, they came to Gopal's place. By this time, Vidya, Pavani, and Uma were grown up enough to bond with each other. They were completely busy with fun, games, storytelling, and conversations. Srinivas's son also joined them. My nephew Nagesh came to visit us with his wife and daughter. We had great family time.

Both Vidya and Uma wanted me to play with them and tell them stories all the time. Uma did not like losing in games; she would get upset. So, I would have to ensure that she always won. Vidya loved playing in the front yard, which had a nice wooden jhoola. So, we use to spend some time there as well. There was a kids' playhouse in the yard, which was once blown off by a big gale. Gopal's office staff came and helped erect it again. The kids would coerce me to bring down jars of snacks and cookies that were kept in a high place as they couldn't reach them.

Apart from playing with me, they wanted to listen to my stories. I narrated an incident about when Uma was a baby. Gopal was in Toledo town near Chicago; he was doing his MBA there. One day he called me and said that we should immediately go into the basement. A tornado had hit a nearby area and it may come to our side as well. Its impact was expected to be devastating. We followed his instructions and went into the basement. Luckily, Toledo was not affected. The girls listened to my story with rapt attention.

Svikriti was growing up to be a good painter. She wanted canvas boards in different sizes. So, Gopal took me to the market and we selected a few, bought them, and presented them to her. She used them for her paintings, one of which still hangs in our house in Navi Mumbai.

Here, too, I continued going for my long morning walks. There were enough areas to explore, some with thick vegetation and some concrete roads. I would go down different roads every day and try to cover the maximum area. The marketplace was a little far away, so I would go there only once in a while as I had to cross a highway with heavy traffic.

We celebrated Uma's birthday on June 24th; Radhika's parents, Srinivas and his family joined us.

We were in the U.S. for over three months this time. Apart from playing with the kids, I read many books from Gopal's extensive collection; The first book I read was A Short Guide to a Happy Life by Anna Quindlen, a columnist for Newsweek. The second one was the 100 Simple Secrets of Happy People by David Niven, a social scientist and a psychologist. I also read the Bhagavad Gita, translated and with a preface by Eknath Easwaran, the founder of the Blue Mountain Center for Meditation in Northern California.

I loved reading The Art of Happiness (A Handbook For Living) by His Holiness the Dalai Lama and Howard Cutler. Tenzin Gyatso, the 14th Dalai Lama, is the spiritual and temporal leader of the Tibetan people. His tireless efforts for promotion of human rights and world peace have brought him international recognition.

I also read Three Cups of Tea by Greg Mortenson and David Oliver Relin. It's based on a real-life experience which motivated the author to build schools in the most backward region of Pakistan. In 1993, Mortenson, a mountaineer, chanced upon an impoverished Pakistani village in the Karakoram Mountains after a failed attempt to climb Mount K2 in the Himalayas. Moved by the inhabitants' kindness, he promised to return and build a school in Korphe, Pakistan. Three Cups of Tea is the story of his promise and its extraordinary outcome.

Mortenson has written another book, Stones into Schools. This is the story of his promise to construct a school in an isolated pocket called Bozai Gumbaz in the Pamir Mountains in Afghanistan. Mortenson could not build that school before constructing many others, and he tells the story in this dramatic new book.

I also read Leaving Microsoft to Change the World by John Wood, the founder of an NGO named Room to Read. Wood worked in Microsoft from 1991 to 1999. In 1998, he took a vacation that changed his life. Trekking through a remote Himalayan village in Nepal, he struck up a conversation with a school teacher who invited him to his school. Here, Wood discovered that there were just 20 books being shared by 450 students. They requested him to send them some books. This put him on a new life path. He left Microsoft at the age of 35 and started the NGO, focused on children's literacy. I also read The World is Flat by Thomas L. Friedman. The book is a brief history of the 21st century; it discusses the Bangalore IT hub, call centres, and how the employees acquired American accents and business techniques in software labs. Another book I read was Presidential Courage by Michael Beschloss, which discusses brave leaders and how they changed America during 1789-1989.

Gopal's collection had a brilliant multiple biography entitled the Team of Rivals: The political genius of Abraham Lincoln by Doris Kearns Goodwin. The book is a biographical portrait of Lincoln and some of his men. It explores how his political acumen shaped the most significant presidency in U.S. History. He forged a team that included his rivals and preserved the nation and freed it from the curse of slavery. Another interesting book was Genghis Khan and the Making of the Modern World by Jack Weatherford.

We returned to India after three-and-a-half-months, filled with happy memories of children, grandchildren, and the times spent with them and with others.

Some anxious moments

ৡৢ

L ife, as they say, is not a bed of roses. There are times when we are faced with situations that leave us fraught with worry, anxiety, and tension. Though I've had a fairly smooth life, I too have had to grapple with a number of such problems. Some of them passed off without causing any damage to our lives, while some others had far-reaching consequences for us. I remember a few such instances from the time of our stay in Mumbai and later.

In 1965, a month after I joined RBI, there was a major suburban railway accident at the Matunga Road station. Two trains coming from opposite directions crashed head-on and some compartments ripped open. Many people died in the accident, which took place in the early hours of the morning. At the time, I was staying in a guest house near the Matunga Road station. I, along with some friends, used to take Central Railway trains instead of Western Railway ones. My father read the news of the crash and sent me a telegram immediately as he was worried for my safety. I replied saying I was safe; the accident had taken place a few hours before my usual morning commute to the office. I later wrote him a detailed letter explaining the situation. Western Railway allowed us to travel by their suburban trains for a couple of days till the tracks were repaired. The incident caused quite some anxiousness among commuters and left my father worried.

Soon after my wife moved to Mumbai, there was a huge earthquake that left everyone shaken. We were staying in a ground floor flat in Thane; the flat belonged to a friend of mine. One day, around 4:30 am, I woke up and suddenly the lights went out. There was a deafening sound coming from beneath the ground and from the surrounding areas. My wife also got up and both of us stood together in the pitch dark, listening to the rumbling. I realised right then that it was an earthquake. The noise stopped after a while, but the electricity did not come back immediately. All our neighbours had gathered with torchlights outside and were discussing what had just happened. Finally, we got to know that there had been a massive earthquake with the Koyna Dam as the epicentre.

Later that day, people started sharing their experiences of the earthquake. One of the residents told us that his young son was sleeping on the floor by the side of a steel cupboard. The cupboard started shaking violently during the earthquake, so he put his weight against it and held on to it tightly so it wouldn't fall on his son. All of us wondered why it did not occur to him to remove the boy from the spot instead of trying to stop the cupboard from falling. We realised that he probably panicked and was not thinking clearly, which is only natural. Next day, we read in the newspapers about the damage wreaked by the earthquake and thanked God that we'd been spared any harm.

Another such incident occurred in 1971 when the Bangladesh Liberation War was on. Bombay was on high alert. There were frequent blackouts, air raid sirens booming day and night, and high security everywhere. I was trained as a warden as well as in firefighting. My bank appointed me as the warden of our data processing department located in our Byculla office. According to instruction, we moved all the cupboards with important documents to the basement. We only kept the essential papers in the office upstairs, which, too, were to be taken to the basement in the event of an air raid siren. I had also been asked to report any potential fire hazards.

We were staying in a third-floor flat in Ghatkopar at that time. Our eldest son was just three years old. For private buildings, the instructions were that during air raid sirens, those staying in terrace flats should ensure their children go underneath a cot to protect themselves in case the ceiling caved in. We had a sturdy iron bed and we made a temporary bed beneath it for Surya. I used to go to the BARC for my computer work. It was well protected with anti-aircraft guns on the hills and on the seaside. All the citizens of Bombay were alert and any suspicious-looking person was reported to the police, including one from near our head office. It took some time for things to come to normal, and we had many sleepless nights.

Once when our second son, Gopal, was about one-and-ahalf years old, he got loose motions. Our family doctor treated him and he seemed to be better, so I went to work the next day. I had to go to our computer installation at the BARC and had a long commute as I had to take a bus—no outside buses/cars were allowed inside. By the time I reached the office, I received a phone call that Gopal's condition had worsened. He had to be admitted to the hospital. I rushed back home, but it took very long as I had to first take the BARC bus to the main gate and then a BEST bus to go home. No taxis were available.

I reached Ghatkopar and got the message that he had been admitted to Rajawadi Municipal Hospital, so I went there. He was being administered saline through a tube in his stomach. He was somewhat stable, but the hospital wasn't very clean and didn't have good facilities. On enquiring from our family doctor, I came to know of a private nursing home in Ghatkopar West which was well-equipped and had good doctors. I shifted Gopal there. We brought him back when he had fully recovered.

The daily charges at that hospital were Rs. 275, an astronomical amount at that time. Some of our friends wondered how I could spend so much on Gopal's treatment—they thought I was either rich or crazy. I was neither. It's just that for me, my boy's health was the top priority.

At one point in time, my younger brother and wife used to stay with us. They moved to a separate accommodation nearby after they had their first child. Once, my sister-in-law had typhoid, so they came to stay with us as they needed help in looking after the baby. My brother's in-laws were also visiting from their village, Madiki. Our house was packed with people—six adults, four children, and a baby. It was full of activity and there was loads of housework to be done. Luckily, my wife was an excellent host and always ensured that the guests were comfortable. She had a huge workload for many days, but she never complained.

Once my sister-in-law recovered, all of them went to Madiki. But the strain of days of excess work had taken a toll on my wife. She had severe cramps all over her body. Our doctor advised that we admit her to the hospital immediately. Her recovery was slow. I had to take care of the children, go to the hospital, and manage work as well. It was really tough. It was a blessing that I was good at cooking and that all my three children were attached to me, so I could manage them fine. In the midst of all this, one of my wife's friends, who was helping me take care of the kids, fell ill on seeing my wife's condition. Now I had no help at all. Luckily, she recovered soon. But we had to go through an entire month of stress, both mental and physical, in managing the situation. The incident also drained us financially for a bit.

Soon after we shifted to my bank's residential quarters in Jalada, Prabhadevi, Surya had a minor accident. One day, when the boys were playing with their friends, a dog started chasing Surya. He ran as fast as he could to avoid the dog. In the process, he fell down and hurt his head. He had a deep cut and needed seven stitches but he put up a brave face. We were worried about the long-term impact of the wound. Luckily, the cut healed with regular medication and dressing and Surya was left with just a scar to show for it. We were amazed at his resilience.

Another such incident I remember was when my wife was unwell and needed to be operated on; I had a tough time balancing my work and personal life. RBI had been given the task of projecting financial savings during the Sixth Five Year Plan (1980-1985). A committee was formed with the deputy governor (DG) as the head. My boss was also on the committee and I was assisting him. It was a very important assignment.

My wife had an ear problem that aggravated around that time. I showed her to a specialist as suggested by RBI doctor. The specialist said that she needed a surgery and had to be admitted immediately to the Bombay Hospital, otherwise, her condition would deteriorate. I was worried about my work but had no choice except to take leave to attend to her. I explained the situation to my boss and requested him to grant me leave for a few days. He flatly refused and told me that he would reject my leave even if I applied for it.

However, he gave me an option—I could go to office either in the morning or after 12 noon and do my work, taking one half of the day off. It was a good offer. In the morning, I would prepare the kids for school and cook breakfast and lunch. I would then send them to school, pack lunch for my wife, and go to the hospital. I would stay there until the doctor came on his rounds and then go to work. At 7:30-8:00 pm, I would leave office and go to the hospital, spend some time with my wife, and return home. One of my colleague's wife would take care of the kids after their return from school. After a few days, my wife was discharged from the hospital; she had recovered well. It was a tough time, but we got through it. When the DG came to know how I had managed to work through a personal crisis, he complimented me.

I, too, have had some health scares. One time, I and a colleague had gone to Tirumala for a site visit of an upcoming project nearby. After we finished our work, we went to pay our respects to Lord Venkateswara at the Tirupati Temple. We had gone for the Suprabhata Seva Darshan or the pre-dawn service. Even as we were waiting for a darshan of the lord, I became unconscious and fell down. People around me picked me up and made me lie down. After a few moments, I regained consciousness, but couldn't immediately recollect where I was. Once I realised I was in the temple, I stood up for a darshan of the Lord. The organisers and my colleague were worried about me, but I was absolutely fine after that and completed my darshan.

In 1994, I was diagnosed with a cardiac problem. It probably first started in 1992, when I was posted at IDBI's Calcutta regional office then. Every day, I used to go for a morning walk and do the Sandhyavandanam in the evening. I continued my routine in Calcutta for about one-and-a-half years. However, from January 1994 onwards, I became irregular with my walks and also my

A Father's Legacy

evening ritual. One day, when I was walking to a Standard Chartered Bank branch nearby, I felt heaviness in my chest. When it continued for a few days, I consulted our Bank doctor. He conducted some tests like ECG and echocardiogram, but there were no anomalies in the reports.

In the meantime, I was transferred to the head office in Bombay in June 1994. I consulted the Bank doctor there. He suspected some blockage in my arteries and referred me to a cardiologist. I was made to undergo a stress test, which I failed, and an angiography was recommended. The results showed 90 percent blockage in one artery and 60 percent in another. At that time, angioplasty wasn't much advanced in India. Balloon angioplasty was available, but its success rate was very low. If it failed, I would need an immediate bypass surgery, which could be risky. The doctor recommended an open-heart bypass surgery for me.

By this time, Surya and Lakshmi's wedding dates had been fixed for August 21st and 24th respectively in Kakinada. Gopal had secured admission to an M.S. in a US university and had to leave by end-August. So, we requested the doctors to postpone the surgery till after the weddings. They agreed reluctantly, advising me not to exert myself much in this condition. My wife and I decided not to tell anyone that I was not well. We didn't want to mar our kids' happiness. Accordingly, she took charge and executed the weddings. Everything went off smoothly.

In September, I met the Bank doctor and told him I was ready. He spoke to the cardiologist and fixed the date for my surgery. We planned the surgery well, delegating tasks within the family. My wife was to remain with me; Surya would organise blood and take care of other arrangements. My daughter and daughter-in-law would interact with the doctors, nurses, and other staff.

I was taken to the theatre and junior doctors administered anaesthesia on me. They tried to make me laugh by saying I would be like a 30-year-old man after the surgery. I joked and said that might be a problem as I might want to marry again. They laughed and I passed out.

The operation was successful. The next morning, when I was in the intensive care unit (ICU), the nurse asked me to open my eyes as I had a visitor. I was still drowsy, but happy to see my wife smiling down at me. After two weeks, I was discharged from the hospital, hale and hearty.

I had another health scare on our long tour of north India. We had returned from Amritsar via Kurukshetra and Delhi and arrived in Vijayawada. I hadn't been feeling hungry for the previous two days and was mostly having liquids. From there we took a train to Rajahmundry. When the train reached the Godavari bridge, I suddenly started feeling uneasy and passed out. Luckily, there were four doctors in our compartment. They had gone to a medical camp near Agra and were returning to Vizag, their headquarters. They administered some first aid and I regained consciousness. We thanked the doctors and got off at Rajahmundry.

But soon, I was ill again and threw up. I felt unwell throughout our taxi ride to Atreyapuram. By now, I had started suspecting that I had come down with jaundice. I spoke to my brother, who was a doctor, and he recommended some medicines. But there was no improvement in my condition. My brother asked me to come to Kakinada immediately and arranged for an appointment with Dr. I.V. Rao, a well-known physician there. I was diagnosed as having stones in my gallbladder. The doctor said I had to be operated on. Although Dr. Rao wanted me to undergo the surgery in Kakinada, I decided to get it done at Global Hospital in Hyderabad, which upset him. However, I went to Hyderabad and was operated on by Dr. Ravindranath at Global Hospital there. I returned home soon after.

On one of our pilgrimage trips after my retirement, we had a very unusual experience. We had gone to Gaya to perform the Pinda Pradanam Karya Kramam (a ritual for the peace of our ancestors). After performing all the rituals, we took a bath in the Vaitarani river. Next, we went for a darshan of the Mangal Gauri Devi temple, one of the yoga peethas. We had to park our car and climb a small hillock to get to the temple. A guide accompanied us and explained the Sthala Mahatyam.

After a darshan of the goddess, my wife started chanting some stotras and making a pradakshina of the temple, while I walked away from the temple to explore the surroundings. When I returned, she was not there. The guide and I searched for her but could not find. We checked the car, but she hadn't gone back there either. The driver also joined the search party.

We stopped a passerby who was coming up the hill, and describing how my wife looked, enquired whether he had seen anyone who looked like her. He said that he had indeed seen a woman of her description walk down the hill. The guide rushed down the path and found her. He brought her back to the car and we headed back to our hotel. Strangely, she did not react to the fact that she had gone missing for a while and we had almost lost her. I feel she had probably gone into a trance after her spiritual experience at the temple.

Trespassing into social activities

౫

The urge for philanthropy ran in my blood. I had witnessed my father's contribution to the Indian Freedom Struggle and to the uplift of Atreyapuram. I had heard of his preceding generations giving back to society. Inspired by them, I too had always been associated with social and religious causes in a small way.

So, in 1986, when one of my friends advised me to involve myself more formally in social work, I gave it a serious thought even though I was preoccupied with my professional and academic pursuits. I decided that I wanted to be associated with the Andhra Education Society, but I wasn't a member. When I told my friend this, he suggested that I get involved with Vivek Granthalaya, a Prabhadevi-based organisation that was spreading the importance of education and literacy among textile mill workers. They ran a library, a Balwadi (a preschool for poor children), and a night school. They got funds from government grants and by raising small donations from individuals and institutions.

I joined the Granthalaya and was made the general secretary. The library and the balwadi were functioning smoothly. So, I paid more attention to the night high school, Sandeepani Ratra Vidyalaya. The headmaster was a committed and sincere person. Many students were finding it difficult to pay their fees because of a textile mill strike (they were mill workers' kids and their parents were not getting their salaries). I arranged freeships for some students. I also instituted some scholarships in the name of my parents. I approached income tax officials, bankers, customs officers, and private sector executives for funds, many of whom were happy to help us. Our efforts enabled many students to complete high school; some of them even went on to join colleges.

We also helped students of some Telugu-medium schools being run by the Brihanmumbai Municipal Corporation (BMC). The BMC was operating about 45 schools. There are many Telugu schools across Maharashtra. A major problem all of them were facing was lack of enough textbooks. The Granthalaya decided to do something about it and got in touch with the then Andhra Pradesh government. In this regard, we met the then chief minister Shri. N.T. Rama rao. He promised all possible support and instructed the education minister to help us. On another trip, we met the officials of the International Telugu Association. They were planning to hold an International Telugu Conference in Kuala Lumpur, Malaysia, and invited us; two of our members attended the seminar.

We also helped upcoming Telugu writers and poets in Bombay publish their work. For this purpose, we launched a quarterly magazine named Mahandhra under the editorship of Shri. S.M.Y. Sastri garu, a renowned writer who had retired as the deputy municipal commissioner of the BMC. He agreed to be the editor after briefing us about the difficulties of running such a publication. We published the magazine for some time and it received a good response in terms of contributions of articles, poems, etc. But after I was transferred to Ahmedabad, there was no one to manage it. The Andhra Mahasabha ran it for some time, but they had to discontinue it because of some problems.

The Granthalaya was getting grants from the Andhra Pradesh government and was able to afford one room in a building thanks to these grants. We later acquired another room in the same building to expand our activities. With the efforts of the chairman and the board of trustees, the Granthalaya was allotted a plot measuring two-and-a-half acres by the BMC to start an engineering institution. Unfortunately, we couldn't make much progress on the project and the municipality eventually took back the plot.

Some friends suggested that I participate actively in the Bombay Andhra Mahasabha, which was involved in a wide range of activities. Often, social organisations are not meticulous about housekeeping and financial activities like writing vouchers, maintaining a book of accounts, depositing money in banks timely etc, because of which auditing their accounts becomes a problem. The Mahasabha was facing similar problems. I thought about the invitation and I agreed. I was elected as a committee member and then appointed as the treasurer. I put processes in place to ensure all financial transactions were recorded and carried out properly. I also ensured that each managing committee meeting discussed and approved them. There were some misappropriations, mainly because of the inefficiency of the manager, and appropriate action was taken against him. This substantially improved the functioning of the Mahasabha and increased its income.

The year passed by and, soon, election for new a managing committee was due. My supporters felt I should continue my services as general secretary of the Mahasabha and put all systems and procedures on a sound footing. I agreed. But some people who had been associated with the organisation for long felt that I was too strict and opposed my candidature. They were backing some other members for the post of president and general secretary. I did not take the matter to heart—it was up to them to decide whether or not they needed my services. As expected, the opposition team won. I was relieved in a way as I felt that unless there was cooperation from all the members, it would not be possible for me to deliver things.

However, within six months, an unexpected development took place. There was some problem and the new committee became non-functional. Some of my well-wishers in the Mahasabha came to me and said they had decided to dissolve the committee and elect a new one. They had identified the presidential candidate as well; he was a nice man and was well known to me. They wanted me to be the general secretary. After a detailed talk with the presidential candidate and some others, I agreed to their proposal.

The new managing committee chalked out an action plan. We decided to plan cultural or other activities on all four Saturdays of the month. One Saturday, we would hold the managing committee meeting, and another there would be a cultural program. There were many Telugu writers in Mumbai, and to encourage them, we thought of organising a Sahitya Gosti on the third Saturday. On the fourth Saturday, we decided to hold a Vignana Peetham and invite eminent Telugu personalities from various reputed organisations to come to the Mahasabha and deliver lectures. The president was very enthusiastic about all the programmes and so were all the other members.

One of the first things I did was start putting a system in place—having a book to record the minutes of each meeting and getting them approved in the next meeting; getting the accounts approved; getting approvals for the estimated expenditure for each programme, particularly cultural ones etc. Soon, the processes fell in place and everything was going well.

The vice-president was a dynamic person as well and ensured that we diversified into different activities instead of doing only routine programmes. Local talent received a lot of encouragement from us.

Sahitya Gosti was a big success. We started with inviting local writers and, soon, writers from other places, particularly from Hyderabad, started showing interest in the event. One time, we invited popular Telugu women writers. The event was very well-received. Our literary activities gained so much momentum that in later years the Mahasabha organised an event entitled Satavadhanam featuring an eminent author from Tirupati. The other cultural activities were also a big hit.

We once organised an Ugadi Sammelanam and also held an annual drama competition and all Telugu associations across Mumbai & Suburbs were invited to participate. Two fundraising campaigns launched by us were also highly successful. The first one was held in the Shanmukhananda hall and the second one was held on the Mahasabha premises. It coincided with the inauguration of our new auditorium.

In the midst of all the successful and good work we were doing, there was an unpleasant episode. Some years ago, the then board of trustees and the managing committee decided to construct a stage and an indoor auditorium on the Mahasabha premises. But, the BMC authorities did not give them permission for an indoor auditorium; they then applied for an indoor badminton court and got permission for the same. Later, they converted the court into an auditorium. They also built a big stage outside and used it as an open-air auditorium. The entire work took a long time because of recurrent design changes and because the people entrusted with the job did not devote sufficient time to it. There was also a big cost overrun.

In the annual general meeting (AGM), there was anger and uproar and allegations were raised that funds had been misused. The AGM appointed an inquiry committee into the allegations. During the probe it was found that there were major financial anomalies. Some of our well-wishers held discussions with members of the previous committee and some contractors. The contractors agreed to return some of the money. Although some members were insisting that we should take strict action in this regard, it was decided that once the contractors returned the money, the case would be closed.

Around the time I was completing two years at the Mahasabha, I was transferred to Ahmedabad by IDBI. I would still visit the Mahasabha whenever I was in Mumbai. On one such visit, I attended the Ramayana dance ballet of Smt. Hema Malini at Nehru Centre. The late Telugu film actor Nageswara Rao and Hindi film actress Smt. Rohini Hattangadi were also guests at the event. I was asked to compère the programme. I was also happy to come from Ahmedabad and participate in the SatavaDhanam by Dr. Medasani Mohan.

After spending some years in Ahmedabad, Calcutta, and Hyderabad on official postings, I returned to Mumbai. The Mahasabha approached me again, asking me to renew my association with them. I was grateful for the offer and readily accepted it.

This time, I was made the secretary of the board of trustees. Unfortunately, I soon realised that all was not well with the workings of the Mahasabha. There were groups within the board of trustees and the managing committee. Thus, even though funds were available and there was work to be done, not much was achieved.

A plot of land was allotted to the Bombay Andhra Mahasabha and Gymkhana by the efforts of Shri. S.M.Y. Shastri Garu, who was the deputy municipal commissioner of the BMC. Unfortunately, the members could not enjoy full benefits of the land. Because the Mahasabha was not very active, the front half of the plot was reallotted to Poddar College for its sports activities. So, the space available reduced by almost half. I hope future members can utilise the area and get better facilities.

In 1992, soon after I had moved to Calcutta to join our regional office there, some members of the Andhra Association, Calcutta, came to meet me. I had met some of them in Bombay through the Mahasabha. They briefed me about their activities and requested me to attend one of their managing committee meetings. At the meeting, I was co-opted as a member. At that time, the president was a woman; she was the wife of RBI manager of the Calcutta office. Soon, I was also made vice-president of the association. The association had some good members and organised regular socio-cultural activities. However, like most such organisations, it was embroiled in legal problems as some members had gone to court over some issue. The state government had appointed two observers in this regard.

At the next AGM, I was appointed president. After I took over my responsibilities, the state government nominees met me and assured their cooperation. Many bankers were associated with the Andhra Association. Most of them came to Calcutta on job postings and spent a few years there.

Until then, our cultural programmes were mostly limited to Kuchipudi dances. After I became president, the members expressed a desire that we organise different types of events on the lines of the Bombay Andhra Mahasabha. So, we came up with programmes like Bhuvana Vijayam, Mutyala Sala, and some plays, musical events etc. The association had some funds and we could have financed the events on our own. But I decided to save the funds for other activities. Instead, I leveraged my personal and professional network to get the support of industrialists who were keen on helping social causes. Without me having to ask, they volunteered to help us by providing necessary support in terms of finances, transportation, etc.

At that time, the governor of West Bengal was a well-known and dynamic politician from Andhra Pradesh who had earlier served as a Union minister. We met him and invited him as the chief guest to one of our Bhuvana Vijayan programmes by Srimatha peetham, headed by Dr. Prasadaraya Kulapati. At his felicitation, I recited a poem. The governor was so impressed that he took out his garland, put it around me, and embraced me. He was a very tall man and I am quite short, so it made for a comic sight. The audience ended up laughing and applauding at the same time. The governor later asked me to visit his house with my wife as he could not come to our place due to protocol. We met several times and discussed the prospects of industrial development in West Bengal. What I liked about the programmes in Calcutta was that all the attendees would pay attention and observe silence during the event.

The Srinadha Peetham team wanted to see Calcutta, particularly the Metro railway, which at that time, was the only metro rail in the country. I personally showed them around the city; they expressed their happiness and gratitude at my gesture.

A popular Hindi writer who was also the president of the Hindi Sahitya Parishad used to attend many of our functions. He was earlier the editor of the Hindi edition of Chandamama.

In one of our literary programmes, we invited eminent Telugu writer Dr. Ravuri Bharadwaja. He presented us with his popular work Pakudu Rallu, written by him. The programme was a great success. I later invited him to my house and he was impressed by our hospitality, and particularly by my wife's warmth.

The Andhra Association ran a primary and high school, which were headed by a competent women headmistress and principal respectively. They used to invite my wife as a guest to their functions. We would help the needy students in various ways.

Once I visited Titagarh in North 24 Parganas for an official visit. The Telugu community was running a school and a library there. They had organised a function where the local MLA was the chief guest. When I started speaking in English, he insisted that I speak in Telugu; I acquiesced. They showed me their library and I donated a small amount of money for it, which made them very happy.

After staying in Calcutta for two years, I was transferred back to Mumbai. The Andhra Association members had developed great affection for me and were sad to see me leave.

Back to my janmabhoomi

ॐ

My attachment to my ancestral village, Atreyapuram, had not diminished despite my having lived away from it for many years. I left Atreyapuram at a very young age and had good memories of the time I had spent there under parental care. I always wanted to go back to Atreyapuram after my retirement. I'd sometimes express my wish to my friends in Mumbai, but I'm not sure they believed me. Probably because I had a very good life in Mumbai too—I had a great career, a wonderful family, children who grew up to be well-educated and loving people, and we had a fulfilling social life with a large circle of friends. We lived in a very comfortable duplex house in Navi Mumbai. There really wasn't much more I could ask for.

Retirement was a long way off and I was busy with my career and family life, especially focussing on our children's education, so there was no question of settling down in Atreyapuram at that time and, therefore, we never thought about it. In fact, after my father's demise in February 1976, my visits to the village reduced substantially. This was because my mother moved into my younger brother's house a few years after my father passed away. After that, I did not get a chance to visit my village for 14-15 years. I visited Atreyapuram in 1994 to invite some of my relatives to my children's weddings in Kakinada in August that year.

Things were running smoothly back in the village as my youngest brother was taking care of our house, which we had rented out to some tenants, and my elder brother was looking after our ancestral land in Atreyapuram and in Kundur. Besides, I was told that my nephew (elder brother's third son) who was doing his M.Sc., may work as a lecturer at the degree college in Atreyapuram, stay in our house, and look after the land. But things did not transpire that way. He refused to work as a lecturer as he did not like teaching and, neither did he want to stay in Atreyapuram.

My mother was a little worried as some people had sent word that they wanted to buy our house. My mother became furious.

My children's education was in an advanced stage and I had to think about their future settlement as well. I acquired a flat at Secunderabad and Kandivli, as and when I had some surplus funds. The rates those days were very low. I acquired 3 plots of land at Hyderabad including one at Banjara Hills. Our employees formed a society with the land allotted by CIDCO. I became a member. I got a duplex house on a 150 square meter, plot in Kalpataru CHS. In due course, we disposed of the Kandivli & Secunderabad flats and the three plots.

During my children's marriages in Kakinada in 1994, discussions came up on how we could retain the house and land in Atreyapuram. But I did not take much interest in the conversation because I was preoccupied with the weddings and my own health problems.

When I was posted at JNIDB in Hyderabad, my mother was staying with me. By this time, my elder brother was not interested in taking care of our house and land in Atreyapuram. So, my younger brother proposed that we dispose of the land. I told my mother that instead of selling it to outsiders, I would purchase the land. But she did not agree to this as there were many stakeholders and she was worried some of them would not cooperate and the deal would be stuck. She suggested we sell the land to outsiders, and eventually if I decided to settle down in Atreyapuram, I could buy land there. I agreed with her.

By 1998, I had decided that we would settle down in Atreyapuram after my retirement. So, I got the house transferred to my name after paying compensation to my brothers and my mother at the rates prevailing at that time. I also decided to buy some land in due course, nearer to the time of my retirement, and shift to Atreyapuram. In due course, I acquired 11.60 acres of land of which 1.79 acres was purchased by Surya.

As my retirement was approaching, I received a few offers for post-retirement work. I wasn't interested in these offers and I politely turned them down. I was extremely busy until the last day of my service and did not leave any work pending when I retired. There was a farewell party for me and my tenure with the bank ended. I was really happy to retire peacefully after nearly four decades of service.

Meanwhile, my Navi Mumbai house was ready. I got the necessary interior work done and we shifted there within a month's time. Utilities like gas connection, telephone, and ration card were all transferred to my new house. After a couple of months, we went to Atreyapuram for a preliminary check in case we shifted there eventually. At that time, we had no intention of moving there immediately or in the near future. But after going there, I felt differently. First, the conditions were much more favourable than we had anticipated. The people in the village were very warm and receptive to us. Second, I did not feel confident that the ryot (cultivator) whose family was handling our agriculture for generations could take care of the operations properly. So, we decided to move there immediately. My wife stayed back and I went to Mumbai to bring all our important documents. Thus, we moved back to my janmabhoomi, Atreyapuram. Surya was working in Mumbai at that time and moved into our house.

Atreyapuram made good progress and developed well since my childhood days, in keeping with the overall development of the state. Atreyapuram became Mandal headquarters having a new building headed by a Mandal Revenue Officer (re-designated as Tehsildar). Atreyapuram Mandal consists of 17 villages. It is well connected with good roads, schools, college, post office, police station, sub-registrar office and banks. Atreyapuram has since become famous for "putareku", a sweet dish introduced by Kshatriya ladies few centuries bank.

The house in Atreyapuram was old and reasonably well maintained. But, it fell short of our needs as it wasn't at par with modern standards. I decided to renovate the house. We constructed a separate block with two bathrooms and two toilets. There was overhead tank with a motor. We installed a new motorised borewell. The pipes were connected to the overhead tank, the kitchen, and four taps so water could be drawn directly. We also installed an Aquaguard water filter for drinking water. In the main house, we totally replaced the flooring with ceramic tiles, plastered the walls, and overhauled the electrical installations with three-phase current. A car garage was also built.

Only part of the house had a false ceiling and wooden flooring; we completed that work so that the house would be cool during summer. We had a tiled roof with a bamboo mesh for support, but it would keep getting spoilt, so I got it replaced with a teak frame. Finally, all the three rooms were fitted with new air conditioners.

We had renovated the entire house so that we and our children, whenever they came to visit, could stay comfortably. I also tended to the garden and revived it. We used to have a malati creeper in the front courtyard. So, I replanted one. We also bought many flowering plants from Kadiyapulanka, which had good nurseries. Everybody admired and appreciated the new look of our house. I named our house Surya Nivas in the memory of my father.

Simultaneously, I concentrated on cultivation. My knowledge of agriculture was outdated. There is no comparison between the agriculture of my childhood and the technologies in place when I moved to Atreyapuram. To begin with, I updated my knowledge by holding discussions with farmers, reading articles in magazines, and watching TV programmes. I also spoke to government officers and visited some farms in far-off places to see what agricultural techniques they were using.

The main crop in the area was paddy and it was rotated with sugarcane, which was sent to the Chelluru sugar factory for crushing. The farmers entered into an agreement with the factory and the money was credited to our bank accounts. We used to sell our paddy to a local trader. We also had around 200 coconut trees. Every 45 days, a trader would come to our farm and arrange for plucking of the coconuts; he would pay us after three to four days at the prevailing rate. Initially, I used to plant banana as an additional crop. Later, I started planting cocoa, which started generating an additional income after three years.

I thought that instead of using the entire land for paddy and sugarcane cultivation, I should look at diversifying. So, on about four acres, I planted coconut and guava trees. Both started giving fruits after two to three years. During this period, I used the land to grow urad dal and sweet corn, both of which gave good returns. Thus, I was doing pretty well as a cultivator. I had one person to assist me on a full-time basis and other labourers were mobilised as and when required. Contrary to the general trend, I benefited from my agricultural operations every year.

My daily routine was more or less fixed, except when I was travelling, mostly to Mumbai, Hyderabad, or abroad. Every morning, I would go to inspect the farms on foot. I would walk on the bunds, carrying a bamboo stick to support myself and to protect against snakes, particularly cobras. They frequent the fields to prey on rats and frogs. But no untoward accident happened to me. Done with the fields, I would plan the day's activities. There were many more tasks to attend to during the day. In the evening, I would drive around in my Maruti 800 and review the day's work and plan for the next day's work. I used to pay the labourers on a daily basis.

Soon after we shifted to Atreyapuram, some Congress workers approached me and requested that I join the party as my family was closely associated with it. They wanted me to become an active member. I politely declined their offer citing my age and my disconnect with the region for such a long time. However, they insisted that I become an ordinary member, which I did.

I also actively participated in the activities of the Rashtriya Swayamsevak Sangh (RSS), Rajahmundry Vibhag. In Mumbai, I had maintained contact with them more at an intellectual level. They used to regularly invite me to their functions, and I had visited their office in Jhandewalan, New Delhi and Kesav Shristi, Bhayander. When I was associated with Rajahmundry Vibhag, I participated in most of the organisation's activities and invited many people to my house. I also gave talks at various places and contributed financially to the RSS.

I was very keen on doing social service for the uplift of my village. Sanitation was a major problem in Atreyapuram, with open defecation leading to unhygienic surroundings. The then government had introduced a scheme for construction of toilets at people's houses, but very few opted for it. Most of the villagers said that they could not afford their part of the contribution, which was very small—it amounted to about 10 days of daily wages at that time. I spoke to the village elders, tehsildar, and the Mandal Parishad Development Office (MPDO) and offered to pay the amount. About 50 families benefited from my contribution of Rs. 25,000. But even after building the toilets, some people were not using them—they were using the toilets to store firewoods and other material! But after we persuaded them, many started using them.

I also undertook a big project to construct a new library building. The existing building was built around 1950 and it was in a dilapidated condition. The library had been started during the freedom struggle around 1930 by my father and some of his friends. It was named Sarada Grandhalayam and was initially housed in a road-facing room in our house. After Independence, it was taken over by the government and shifted to the present building.

Some village elders and the district branch of the Andhra Pradesh Library Association (APLA) came to me for help in constructing a new building. The coming year, 2014, was my father's birth centenary. Contributing to the library seemed an apt way to commemorate his life. So, in September 2013, I agreed to give a donation subject to the condition that the new building be named after my father. They readily agreed. The state government had a scheme known Janmabhoomi for such social projects, under which the donor had to give one-third the cost and the government would pay the remaining funds. The Panchayati Raj department estimated the cost of the building at Rs. 4.5 lakh. So, we had to pay Rs. 1.5 lakh for the construction.

The then MLA called me and gave me some sound advice regarding the library rebuilding project. He said that government estimates tend to be conservative and that under the prevailing construction norms, it would not be possible to complete the building at the estimated cost. He therefore suggested that I should execute the construction project myself as that would help me utilise the funds properly. I readily agreed to his suggestion even though I had no experience in construction. There was a young, dynamic political leader in our area who knew most raw material suppliers. I approached him to help me connect with them. Then I roped in a mason who had experience in building construction and hired another person to assist him in labour supply, material transport, and other works. The old building was demolished and the foundation stone was laid by the APLA chairman and the local MLA.

Just as the MLA had told me, the estimated funds were not sufficient for the project, especially because I maintained a high standard of construction. I spoke to my brother about the matter. The MLA, meanwhile, suggested that the Member of Parliament (MP) from the area could sanction an additional amount through the Members of Parliament Local Area Development Scheme (MPLADS). My brother pursued the matter and I also met the MP a couple of times. He sanctioned Rs. 1.5 lakh from MPLADS and with that money, we completed the building. Our family contribution to the construction amounted to Rs. 2 lakh of which Rs. 1.10 lakh was given by me.

The inauguration of the new library building was fixed for October 16, 2005, at 10:00 am. It was a gala event. All the three MPs of our district, the APLA chairman, the district APLA chairman, local MLA, and other dignitaries attended the function. The building was named Sri Kasichainula Suryanarayana Sata Jayanthi Grandhalayam after my father. The credit for getting government approvals, MPLADS, MPS and other dignitaries for the inaugural function goes entirely to my elder brother who relentlessly pursued the matter. I was very happy to see my dream for my father's birth centenary come to fruition.

We also tried to improve healthcare in Atreyapuram. On the eve of my elder brother's retirement a few years ago, his wellwishers had formed a Trust named Sri Kasichainula Krishna Murti Trust for Healthcare. Incidentally my family contributed Rs. 25,000 to the corpus of the trust. The main aim of the trust was to help people who were in need of medical treatment but couldn't afford it. We conducted three medical camps in the village under the trust. The first one was an orthopaedics and general health camp, the second one was focused on women's health and gynaecology, and the third one was an eye camp.

For the first camp, we had a team of six specialists from Kakinada General Hospital and other hospitals come to Atreyapuram. More than 2,400 people attended the camp and some were recommended to go to Kakinada for further treatment. For the second camp again, six eminent gynaecologists from Kakinada came down to our village and examined more than 2,000 patients. The eye camp was conducted jointly with Kiran Eye Hospital. Free spectacles were provided by the trust to the needy. All the camps provided free lunch, tea/coffee, and medicines. The Medical Shops Association also donated some medicines for distribution in the camps.

Philanthropy was an important part of my family's life, and there were several other occasions on which I tried to play the good samaritan. One of my relatives, who later became Surya's father-in-law, wanted to build a hospital in his village, Aryavatam, also in East Godavari district, in memory of his grandfather. He asked me for a specific donation—200 bags of cement. I agreed, but instead of the raw material, I gave him Rs. 5,000, which was equivalent to the price of 200 cement bags at that time. When the hospital was ready, my contribution was acknowledged.

Another time, my brother-in-law (wife's brother), who was the secretary of the Brahmin Association in Attili, was constructing a building and requested my wife to contribute to the construction of one room. Accordingly, we gave Rs. 30,000 for the purpose.

The local Christian community planned to reconstruct their Church which was in bad shape. They approached me for a donation.

I gave a donation of Rs.25,000/- to them. My mother donated Rs. 15,000 for the construction of an additional classroom in our village college. She also donated Rs. 20,000 for the construction of a Ramalaya. I also contributed towards this. Besides, there were many other smaller contributions made by my family for the welfare of the villagers.

All our children and their families visited us while we were in Atreyapuram and we had great times together. Our grandchildren loved their rural retreats. They would roam around the house and the courtyard. I had set up a jhoola (swing) under the mango tree, and they used to love swinging on it. I would also take them to our farms and they had a rollicking time running around on the open fields. They would be treated to fresh coconut water on the farms. We held a couple of socio-religious functions to introduce my children and grandchildren to the village. My wife was a good host as always, calling people over for lunch, tea, and snacks and giving them gifts.

We celebrated the first birthday of our grandson Vivek in Atreyapuram. Many people were invited to lunch and we gave them gifts. Vedic scholars blessed him. We also celebrated the Annaprasana of our grandson Sriharsh in our house. Our granddaughter Pavani liked music, so I got her a CD player so she listened to songs when she visited us.

I was on excellent terms with local government officials, leaders of political parties, village elders, as well as traders who bought my agricultural produce. For social interactions, I devoted some time to the Rajahmundry branch of the RSS.

Years had passed full of action and satisfaction. Our purpose of moving to Atreyapuram had more or less been fulfilled. I am advancing in age. My children are holding high positions. Grandchildren started schooling and growing up. Thoughts crossed our mind that it was time to relocate to Mumbai, my *karmabhoomi*. Finally, in May 2011, we shifted back to Mumbai after nine years of enjoyable stay in Atreyapuram.

I had fulfilled my long-cherished dream and had no regrets. Some people offered to purchase our land at a reasonably good price. But when I thought of alternate investment options in Mumbai, I decided not to sell the land. The real estate market in Mumbai was not attractive at that time and I had lost my competence in the share market. So, I decided to hold on to the land for some more time.

One thing, however, was left unfinished—we wanted to donate our house to some established religious organisation for the conduct of their activities on a long-term basis. I reached out to an acquaintance who was well-connected with some spiritual organisations and expressed my desire to him.

Coincidentally, around that time, Swami Jayendra Saraswathi of the Kanchi Kamakoti Peetham had come to Rajahmundry to lay the foundation for the renovation work of the Annavaram Sri Satyanarayana Swamy temple. He was also scheduled to inaugurate a Vedic pathashala in Mukkamala village nearby. However, the person who had donated his house met with an accident and the programme was cancelled. The Kamakoti representatives were already in Rajahmundry at that time.

My acquaintance told Swamiji about my offer. Their representative came to our village, took photos and videos of our house, and showed them to Sri Sankara Vijayendra Saraswathi, the junior pontiff of the Kanchi mutt. The swami was impressed by our house and accepted our offer. He instructed the representative to invite my wife and me to Kanchi Peetham immediately. Accordingly, we went to Kanchipuram.

We had a darshan of Sri Jayendra Saraswathi and waited for an audience with Shri Sankara Vijayendra Saraswathi as he was busy with the Chandramouleshwara puja. After coming back to his room, he called us. He enquired whether all our family members were agreeable with our decision. I said yes. He then asked me some questions about our family. Later, he instructed the representative to arrange for our lunch and show us the Kamakshi temple, Sri Chandrasekhara Saraswati University, the golden temple, Veda pathshalas, and other places at the Peetham. It was a very happy and satisfying spiritual journey.

Swamiji informed us that the centre to be opened at our home would be named Anantha Sri Chandrasekhara Saraswathi Swami Anustana Kendram. The date for the inaugural function was fixed for April 25th, 2012, Wednesday, at 10:34 AM.

Swamiji told us that my wife and I should perform the inaugural puja. We immediately went back to Atreyapuram as there wasn't much time and we had a lot to do, from organising a name board, printing invitation cards and flex-banners, to arranging catering. We managed to do all of these things and invited the press for the event. With the blessing of Swamiji, the function went off very well. The media wrote about the centre, highlighting our donation of the property, worth nearly Rs. 20 lakh. The kendram started regular pujas, Veda pathanam, and reciting of the Devi Sahasranamam. A Smartha Pathashala with about eight students was also started on the premises.

Finally, Sri Sri Sri Kanchi Kamakoti Uttaradhikari Sri Sri Sri Sankara Vijayendra Saraswathi Shankaracharya came to our house on July 11th, 2015, a Saturday. My wife, our eldest son, and I received him with poornakumbham. He blessed the house and all the people present. The visit coincided with Godavari Maha Pushkaram, and therefore we felt doubly blessed. Swamiji invited us to Gospada Kshetram, Kovvuru; the very next day, we went there, participated in the activities, and received the prasadam.

I was very happy that my dream had been fulfilled. My father's name lives on in the form of a library and the Kanchi Kamakoti centre at our ancestral house in Atreyapuram.

Relocation to karmabhoomi

ॐ

After we decided to shift back to Mumbai, it took me almost two years to wrap up things in Atreyapuram and implement the decision. I got our tenant to vacate our Navi Mumbai house, got it painted, refurbished, and finally returned to the megapolis on May 27th, 2011. It was a duplex house with a built-up area of 1,637 square feet. The ground floor housed the hall, kitchen, and one bedroom, and there were two bedrooms and a sit out on the first floor. We also had a terrace and a kitchen garden. The front entrance had a garage and above it was a balcony. The society, Kalpataru CHS Ltd, was promoted by IDBI staff. It had 16 duplex houses and other two and three bedroom flats.

The actual resettlement did not take much time. I got a landline telephone and transferred my driving licence to Navi Mumbai RTO from Rajahmundry. I disposed of my Maruti 800 in Atreyapuram. In Mumbai, I bought a Maruti Zen Estilo in a coffee colour, which was fashionable then.

I transferred my IDBI bank account from the Rajahmundry branch to the CBD Belapur branch in Mumbai, along with my fixed deposits. I got the gas connection and our voter identity cards transferred as well. In due course, I got my Aadhaar card transferred and applied for a new one for my wife as the old one was non-functional. Thus, we resettled quickly and reestablished contacts with all our old friends. My son Surya and his family were in Mumbai to help us whenever required.

The first social function we organised after moving back to Mumbai was the Sashti Poorti (completion of 60 years) of my wife in 2012. The second major function we celebrated was our grandson Sriharsh's Upanayanam in the society community hall. We also celebrated our 50th marriage anniversary on June 18th, 2017. Although our marriage date was April 26, we deferred the celebration date for the convenience of our children and grandchildren. We continue to celebrate Ganesh Chaturthi and Deepavali every year with Surya's family in Mumbai.

There have, however, been some significant changes in our social life. In Atreyapuram, every day was hectic with loads of tasks to be done and people coming to meet us all day long. Here, our lives are relatively quieter as most of the people are from different social backgrounds and age groups. But we have settled back into city life.

With new routines and different priorities, life is always enjoyable. We're leading a nice, quiet retired life. I go for morning walks to a place known as Mango Garden, where I meet many people. Sometimes, I visit a far-off valley with a couple of former colleagues. I also do the grocery shopping, apart from reading newspapers and watching news channels. My wife and I watch a few TV serials in Telugu as well. Occasionally, we'd go over to friends' places or attend social functions.

I go to Atreyapuram every six months to look after the agricultural activities, which are taken care of by a tenant. He pays the rent every year. I also meet all our old friends and acquaintances, with whom I am in regular contact on the telephone.

Retired life has given me the time to read voraciously. Over the years, I had accumulated a large number of books but not had the time to read them. Now, I'm catching up on all the reading. I also take down notes for myself while reading.

I read nine books on Hindu religion and culture written by my maternal uncle, Sri Jatavallabhula Purushottam, in Telugu. Some of them are Bharatiya Vaibhavam, Bharatiya Vignanam, Hindu Matam, Dharma Manjari, Mahakavi Sandesam, Chitrashetakam, and Radio Upanyasullu.

There was also a small booklet on his life from which I learned things about him I did not know—like the fact that he did his

M.A. in both Sanskrit and English. He was also the principal of Sanskrit College at Kavvuru W.G. and a lecturer in Sanskrit at SRR & CVR Government Degree College, Vijayawada and Kakinada. My uncle was also a great orator.

Next, I devoted time to study the Sri Bhagavad Geeta-Yedathatatham in Telugu by Srila Prabhupada, the founderacharya of ISKCON. It was a great spiritual experience. I continue to read the shlokas of the Bhagavad Geeta. It was interesting to learn that the author was not trained in the Vedas.

I also read the 16 Upanishads in two volumes by Advaita Ashrama, Calcutta. The first volume contains the Isa, Kena, Katha, and Taittiriya Upanishads. The second volume contains the Aitareya, Mundaka, Mandukya, Krittika, and Prashna Upanishads. I went through them a number of times so as to deeply absorb some of the ideas.

Among the books I acquired are the two volumes of the Gospel of Sri Ramakrishna. It is an English translation of the Sri Sri Ramakrishna Kathamrita, which recounts the activities and conversations of Sri Ramakrishna Paramhansa with his disciples, devotees, and visitors.

I also read the Complete Works of Swami Vivekananda in eight volumes. They were released in 1998, the 125th birth anniversary of Swami Vivekananda. They contain his writings on the four yogas, epistles, speeches, poetic compositions, etc. Another interesting book I read was Autobiography of a Yogi by Paramahansa Yogananda, who made a mark as a yogi and propagated yoga in the US.

I enjoyed reading Laws of Manu, popularly known as Manu Dharma Shastra. It contains a number of suggestions for a happy, disciplined way of life for individuals and for the society. For an economist like me, Kautilya's Arthashastra in three volumes was enlightening and enriching.

I read a disturbing book called The Accidental Prime Minister: The Making and Unmaking of Manmohan Singh by Sanjaya Baru.

The book describes how the high-level decisions were made not by Singh but by the then Congress President Sonia Gandhi. She had access to all the government files. According to the book, the Prime Minister was just there to implement the decisions.

On all important religious occasions, I perform Sandhyavandanam both morning and evening. On Mahashivaratri, I recite the important Siva Stotram. We also visit temples in the vicinity including the Shiva, Sri Rama, Anjaneya, Vinayak, and Shirdi Sai Baba temples in CBD Belapur, the Iskcon temple at Kharghar, the Sri Kamaskamma, Hanuman, and Sri Rama temples in the SIES College area and the Sri Venkateswara temple at Nerul.

My wife performs her daily puja without fail. We have flowering plants in our garden which she used for her puja.

We are leading a happy and peaceful retired life.

Word of Gratitude

૭૦૨

*I*n this long and eventful journey of more than 75 years, I owe *my success to a number of people. Most important among them are: My elders, who helped lay the foundation of my life with their initial training and constant blessings, my family members, who have always been supportive and eagerly participated in all the activities that interested me, and with whom I share my life and my values; and my friends and well-wishers, who have been there in tough as well as good times. The shortcomings, of course, are all mine. Here, I'd like to take the chance to thank them and express my gratitude to them.*

I'm eternally grateful to my father, who passed on our family values to me, gave me a traditional education, and motivated me to achieve bigger and bigger goals in life. My mother always looked after my welfare and comfort, made sure I was well-fed and taken care of, and taught me how to conduct myself in difficult situations. She also impressed upon me the importance of tirth yatras.

I am thankful to my maternal uncle and aunt, who looked after me so well when I stayed with them for my college education in Kakinada. I learnt a lot from them about cleanliness, prudence, hard work, and other virtues valued by society.

My elder brother always wanted me to be an achiever. He motivated me, helped me plan my future, and encouraged me in every respect, including providing financial support during my education. My sister-in-law was a source of strength for me and always wished me well. I am also thankful for their contribution towards the weddings of my son and daughter in Kakinada; they played a key role and supported us as if their own children were getting married. My brother also always stood by us whenever we had any health problems. Just a phone call from him would help me relax.

I am thankful to all my other brothers and sisters who treated me so well in childhood and also my children whenever we visited their houses.

My wife's contribution to my life is unsurpassable. She came into my life at the young age of 16 years. From a small village, she landed in Mumbai, a huge, fast city, where everyone was a stranger and the language and culture very different. But she picked up Hindi fast and adapted remarkably to her new life. She conducted herself with much dignity and was well liked by all we met. She was a good host, always cheerful, and never thought any ill of others. She always welcomed people who needed a kind word or a warm gesture to our house. Thanks to her, our house was always full of guests.

She never complained when I couldn't devote enough time to her or to our children due to office exigencies and academic pursuits. She always supported me in carrying out my responsibilities towards my close relatives, never protested whenever I had to financially support any of them. She gladly accepted my responsibilities as her own.

During the weddings of our son and daughter, when I was suffering from a heart ailment, her strong character and boldness was on display. She took full charge of the situation and made sure that both the functions went off smoothly and were memorable. And we didn't let anyone know that I wasn't well, so it wouldn't mar their happiness or the festivities. She executed both the weddings beautifully.

She proactively organised social and religious functions and celebrations in our house, leaving her mark on each event.

It gives me great joy to think that in our long journey of 50 years, we've always been together. The time we've spent apart must amount to less than two years in all.

Our three children had happy childhoods and she supported me in raising them to be well-educated, wellbehaved people who are loved by my relatives, our friends and their own friends.

Our firstborn Surya gave us great joy. He was the blue-eyed boy among my friends, most of whom were not married then. He started talking even before his first birthday. He was very affectionate towards his brother and sister and would always include them in his play. He gradually worked on his academic scores and succeeded in getting admission in a good engineering college. He also secured jobs with his efforts, without depending on my official position.

He has a good heart and is always ready to help people. Once his grandmother was stranded in Pune because of a goof-up by his maternal uncle. He went there and picked her up and brought her to Mumbai. She still remembers the incident. Another time, one of my brother's close friends, who was visiting us, had a heart attack at our place. I had left for work. After informing me, Surya arranged an ambulance and admitted him to the hospital. His prompt action helped save the man's life. Surya showed us around the U.A.E. when he was in Abu Dhabi and made sure we had a nice time in Toronto. He also participated in the programme of Sri Sri Sri Sankara Vijayendra Saraswathi Swamiji at our house at Atreyapuram, showing his commitment to carrying on our family tradition.

Our second son, Gopal was an extrovert since childhood. He always loved being with friends. He took initiative in all spheres and always saw the task through. He was also a good communicator. Therefore, he was popular among our friends and relatives. He was also very focussed on his academics. After completing his engineering from Bangalore, he wanted to go to the US for his M.S. He applied on his own and got admission there at the University of Iowa. When he was in the US, he helped many of his friends from Mumbai and some of my nephews who had gone there for higher education. He made sure we had a lovely time in the US, showing us around during each of our four visits there.

Our daughter Lakshmi was very attached to us as a child and she never went far from home for her studies, unlike her brothers. My wife brought her up as a typical Andhra girl, making her wear traditional dresses, jewellery, and makeup. She was meticulous in every activity, including her studies. She had a small circle of friends, but the few friends she had were very close to her. She earned a good name while working as a pathologist in Calcutta. We eschewed all foreign matches for her as we felt she wouldn't be able to stay too far away from us. So, when she left Mumbai to go to the US, we were worried how she would manage, but she stayed strong. In the US, she improved her qualifications and did an M.S. in Information Technology. Now, she has a large friends' circle. She conducted herself very well at her in-law's place. When both of us visited the US, she took very good care of us. She is very popular among my brothers and sisters as well as in Atreyapuram.

Our son-in-law Prasad is a gentleman to the core and knowledgeable not only in his own field, but also in Sanskrit, Telugu literature, and spiritual topics. He participated actively in the inaugural function while handing over our Atreyapuram house to the Kanchi Kamakoti Peetham and gave an enlightening speech on the occasion. All were impressed by his words. He also showed us many places in the US, particularly the Niagara Falls.

Our two daughters-in-law became part of our family and blended in so well. Everyone remembers them in Atreyapuram for their courteous behaviour and their hospitality.

All my grandchildren are a source of joy for both of us. They too are popular in Atreyapuram, among our relatives, and among our friends in Mumbai. Everyone remembers them from the celebration we had for Sriharsh's Upanayanam. Each one of them is talented in his or her own way. Svikriti is smart and bold and is doing her engineering in the US; she is also a good singer and dancer. Pavani is working on her talent as a Hindustani vocal musician. Uma is growing up as an intelligent girl and has reached the finals of the Spelling Bee competition. Sriharsh and Vivek show great discipline and dedication towards all they do. Their conduct during their Upanayanam ceremony made us proud. Sriharsh picked up Sandhyavandanam in just a few sessions from me. He is so confident, he will be able to recite it on his own after a few more sessions. Vivek is also picking it up well. Vidya is talented and is very wellpresented. She is quite articulate and fashionable.

I am grateful to all our friends, who supported us and helped us during various stages of our life in Mumbai, Hyderabad, Kakinada, Atreyapuram, and Attili among other places.

I am thankful to the residents of Atreyapuram for readily accepting me and extending their cooperation in my activities for improving the facilities and development of the village.

I am grateful to the Kanchi Kamakoti Peetham for accepting my proposal to utilise our house for their spiritual and religious activities.

Family Lineage

ಞಞ

Name of Family Member	Relation to Author	Date of Birth
Shri Kasichainula Suryanarayana	**Father**	15-04-1904
Smt. Kasichainula Laxmi Devamma	**Mother**	18-11-1908
Shri Kasichainula Kameswara Rao	**Self** (Author)	23-05-1942
Smt Kasichainula Sri Bhanumati Devi	**Wife**	14-08-1950
Shri Kasichainula Suryanarayan	**Son**	14-09-1968
Shri Kasichainula Gopal	**Son**	14-11-1970
Smt Lakshmi Nukala	**Daughter**	28-01-1972
Smt Kasichainula Suseela	**Daughter-in-law** (wife of Surya)	10-06-1971
Ms Kasichainula Svikriti	**Granddaughter** (Daughter of Surya & Suseela)	19-02-1996
Mast Kasichainula Sriharsh	**Grandson** (Son of Surya & Suseela)	10-11-2004
Smt Kasichainula Radhika	**Daughter-in-law** (Wife of Gopal)	05-02-1974

A Father's Legacy

Name of Family Member	Relation to Author	Date of Birth
Ms Kasichainula Uma Mihira	**Granddaughter** (Daughter of Gopal & Radhika)	24-06-2003
Ms Kasichainula Vidya Mahimi	**Granddaughter** (Daughter of Gopal & Radhika)	22-10-2006
Shri Nukala Venkata Ramakrishnaprasad	**Son-in law** (Husband of Lakshmi)	01-11-1966
Ms Nukala Pavani Annapoorna	**Granddaughter** (Daughter of Lakshmi & Prasad)	20-09-2000
Mast Nukala Vivek Ramakrishna	**Grandson** (Son of Lakshmi & Prasad)	05-03-2003

My children and grandchildren

Fond Thoughts

My love for my father is out of respect. Respect for the strong values inculcated into the family. Respect for his work ethics. Respect for his social standing at his native village, fragmented on caste and class lines; not only building upon my grandfather's reputation but also enhancing it. Respect for his contributions to his extended family and his attempts to keep them engaged and connected. Respect for the way he has and continues to lead his life.

Migration from rural India to urban cities is not uncommon. However, a very small percentage of such migrants make it to the executive levels, retaining their beliefs & culture while creating a strong identity. This book is the story of a shy village boy who went on to become a highly successful development banker. This story has been written by my father for next generations.

Suryanarayan Kasichainula (Son)

❧ ❦

My father is someone who I've always looked up to. His principled behavior is unmatched by anyone that I've met in my life. He has set an extremely high standard of integrity, courtesy and dignity. Despite a stoic exterior, he is a very kind and generous person who spent a fortune lending a helping hand to his near and dear ones when they were in need. However, true to his principles, he never publicly let it be known lest the recipient of his generosity feel belittled. He expected little else besides courtesy in return, making him a standout gentleman.

Due to his perseverance and innate decency, he has managed to overcome several hurdles in his career and personal life and achieved commanding heights. He can look back with pride on a life well-spent. While chasing his career ambitions, he never forgot his roots. He continued to nurture his passion for the arts, agriculture and simple living. He is extremely detail oriented and rarely leaves anything to chance.

As children we never missed events or were left in the lurch due to sloppy planning. We didn't know the invisible hand at work then, but faced with our own families and the complexity of life, it's apparent how much we owe him for a smooth childhood, free of worry.

As with anything, I'm confident that my father would have done a thorough job of writing a great memoir.

Gopal Kasichainula (Son)

The Nanna (father) I know is a very disciplined, organized and generous man. He has built a character that is exemplary. Despite many challenges and hardships, his determination and meticulous planning have allowed him to fulfill all his responsibilities. Above all, he has built sweet memories for us to cherish.

As a young girl, I would peek through the window watching my Nanna play badminton. He would signal me to come down

A Father's Legacy

when I was ready. I would quickly gulp my breakfast, take my school bag and go downstairs. He would gently hold my hand and walk me to my school. I loved going to school with him because he would never say no to buying treats like cotton candy and he would even carry me to school no matter how tired he was. On one such day, I remember telling him that many of my classmates came to school on two-wheelers, but he should buy a car and drive me to school. It was a casual comment by a little girl. But a few years later we did get our car and that day will always be cherished by me.

During my elementary years, Nanna would wear a limited number of clothes. I would ask why he wouldn't buy more like my friends' dads. He would smile and affectionately tell me that he liked what he wore. Little did I know that he was sacrificing for his family and extended family. At a time when women were required to do all the household duties, my Nanna never hesitated to pick up little chores in order to help my mother. On Sundays, he would sharpen our pencils, cover our books and trim our nails. There were days when he would cook and even wash his own clothes and iron them. Every single day, he would meticulously polish his shoes. Even after he came home tired from work he would get his own glass of water. He wouldn't expect my mom to do it for him. Nanna made weekends very special for us. Certain Saturdays were movie days and certain Sundays were beach days. He would take us to the nearby seashore and buy us Kulfi or some other fun snacks. We would spend time building sand castles.

Hidden behind his strong and stern personality is a very gentle one. I saw it first hand when I was a teenager and had my first surgery. He couldn't bear to see my black and blue scars from the IVs. I also saw it when he came to assist me after the delivery of my son. When I refused to let him do my chores, he reminded me that he was here for a purpose.

Despite the hard work he put in to build and acquire what he now has, he donated a good part of it to a cause without hesitation. In addition, he has also built a library, toilets for the poor and donated to charities in his native place. Clearly, he cares about others. A few words or sentences cannot describe what I truly want to say about my father. But this is an attempt to say what I feel about him.

Lakshmi Nukala (Daughter)

≫ ≪

Tatagaru (Grandfather in Telugu) is a natural storyteller. Sitting in his old-fashioned chair in the center of the living room, he digs into his encyclopedia of knowledge and experiences, completely immersing any listening ear. His powerful presence demands respect. He invariably has the final say, but for good reason. His decisions guarantee comfort for everyone involved. Every visit, he makes sure to reinforce our morale. He expresses his pride in our accomplishments and awards us with his praises and gifts. Evidently, his leadership abilities not only translated into his professional successes but also into becoming the anchor to the Kasichainula family.

Svikriti Kasichainula (Granddaughter)

≫ ≪

When I was a young one, Tatagaru would always bring pastries for Vivek and I. As soon as we would reach Athreyapuram or Mumbai, the first thing he would do is go to the nearby pastry shop to get both of us a box. Excitedly, we would eat up the pastries, and Tatagaru would smile. Evidently, Tatagaru is the type of gentleman to care extremely for others.

Pavani Nukala (Granddaughter)

≫ ≪

Whenever one has a question or needs something Google is found useless. My Tatagaru, a very learned and generous man can answer almost anything and give his insightful opinion.

Vivek Nukala (Grandson)

❊ ❊

Tatagaru (Grandfather in Telugu) is a wonderful role model who is always enjoyable to be around. I've always enjoyed having conversations with him ranging anywhere from favorite foods to economics. One of my fondest memories is sitting in his house in Mumbai after 5th grade and chatting with him about American politics and Indian history. He is someone who will never hesitate to teach me something new and is always patient even if I don't understand it the first time. He shows his love for me and my cousins in many different ways, and we all enjoy spending time with him. The summer before I started high school, we had a family reunion of all of Tatagaru's kids and grandkids. We performed a talent show for him and Maama (Grandmother in Telugu), and even though it was their wedding anniversary, everyone still decided to sing me 'Happy Birthday'. There is never an unhappy moment with my grandfather and we are all extremely grateful to have him in our lives.

Uma Kasichainula (Granddaughter)

❊ ❊

My grandpa is a good man with his way of things. He is kind, sweet and very knowledgeable. He is also very supportive to my thoughts and actions. Speaking to him makes me feel good and I love him a lot. There is a lot of goodness in him and I hope to learn a few of those good things.

Sriharsh Kasichainula (Grandson)

❊ ❊

I love my Tatagaru (Grandfather in Telugu), and I know he loves me back. Whenever I visit him & Maama (Grandmother in Telugu) in India, I feel like I am at home. He praises me, listens to the songs I sing, and tells me what I need to do to be an even better version of myself. I very much enjoy his insightful wisdom, and intriguing stories. He cares about me, and I couldn't have asked for a better Tatagaru.

Vidya Kasichainula (Granddaughter)

A Father's Legacy